FAITH@WORK

What Every Pastor and Church Leader Should Know

"I believe one of the next great moves of God is going to be through the believers in the workplace."

BILLY GRAHAM

D1306943

OS HILLMAN

FAITH @ WORK MOVEMENT
What Every Pastor and Church Leader Should Know
Copyright ©2004 by Os Hillman
Library of Congress Cataloging-in-Publication Data
ISBN 1-888582-13-8

Aslan Group Publishing
3520 Habersham Club Drive, Cumming, GA 30041 USA
678-455-6262

Printed in the United States of America.

DEDICATION

Dedicated to all the shepherds in the body of Christ who serve through the local church and want to equip and commission workplace believers to impact the nations for Jesus Christ.

CONTENTS

CONTENTS

continued

FOREWORD

In my fifty or so years of ministry, most of them spent in helping to lead the body of Christ, I have witnessed a good number of significant paradigm shifts. Clearly, our God is not a defender of the status quo. He constantly brings new times and seasons. He is not static; He is dynamic. Change is simply a way of life in God's kingdom.

Some changes come slowly, others more rapidly. Without question, one of the most rapid paradigm shifts in the church over the past few decades has been the explosive emergence of what has been called the "faith and work movement" or "ministry in the marketplace" or "kings and priests" or "anointing for business," just to list some examples of the emerging terminology. Since I first became focused on this movement in 2001, I have read much of the literature and I have become acquainted with many of the top leaders. The consensus of those who have a much longer track record in the faith and work movement than I do is that, while some origins can be traced back to the 1950s, the rapid acceleration that we are experiencing today began sometime during the late 1990s.

One of the pioneers who for many years patiently and persistently helped to move the body of Christ along the pathway toward understanding marketplace ministries more fully was Os Hillman, the author of this book. I feel honored to have Os as a friend because I admire the work he is doing so much. I think I could argue the point that Os Hillman, at the present time, would have the broadest comprehension of the whole movement of any of its current leaders. The International Coalition of Workplace Ministries that Os leads is the most inclusive network that we have nationally. Hundreds of thousands of people read his *TGIF* on-line daily devotional geared to the working person. As you will see in my reading list that appears toward the end of this book, he is the most prolific writer in the field to date.

All of this superbly qualifies Hillman to author this book, *The Faith@Work Movement*. More than any other book so far, this one attempts to build bridges between, if I may use my personal terminology, "nuclear church" leaders and "extended church" leaders.

Let me explain.

Biblically, the word for "church," *ekklesia*, means "the people of God." God's people are the church, not only on Sunday when they gather together for worship and teaching (the nuclear church), but also on the other six days when they find themselves in the workplace (the extended church). It is becoming increasingly clear that, not only do these two forms of the church really exist, and that each is truly the biblical church, but also that they are quite different from each other, despite the fact that they contain largely the same people.

While simply acknowledging that there is a difference might seem rather innocuous, the situation becomes more complex when we begin to explore the breadth of the gap between the nuclear church and the extended church. According to some respectable research, the gap turns out to be much larger than most people might think. The nuclear church and the extended church each has a distinct culture, and each culture, as cultures do, operates according to its own rule book. Most extended church leaders understand both rule books because they not only function in the workplace, but they also are active in a local church. However, most nuclear church leaders understand only one rule book. This can and does cause some of them to feel very uncomfortable with the notion that their own members customarily function, behind their backs, in a different "church" with different behavior patterns six days a week.

It should go without saying that God's desire in this new season of the faith and work movement is that all His people move forward in harmony. It would be a severe setback to the kingdom of God if nuclear church leaders decided to condemn the rule book of the extended church for whatever reasons, and thereby widen the gap.

Os Hillman is acutely aware of this situation. That is why he wrote *Faith@Work*. This excellent book is designed to bring clear understanding of the workplace to all church leaders. It will go a long way toward helping to bridge the gap between the church and the marketplace. Whether you are a nuclear church leader or an extended church leader or simply a believer who wants to move in the stream of God's new times and seasons, you will greatly enjoy this book.

–C. Peter Wagner

SPECIAL ACKNOWLEDGMENTS

I wish to thank some key individuals who made major contributions to this resource:

Kent Humphreys, my friend and colaborer in the faith at work movement, is president of the Fellowship of Companies for Christ International (FCCI). Kent has a keen understanding of the role workplace believers should play in conjunction with the local pastor. He has graciously allowed me to excerpt one chapter of his book, *Lasting Investments* (Navpress, February 2004).

Doug Spada and David Scott have allowed me to include an article written especially for pastors and church leaders to help them understand the major foundations when considering workplace ministry at the local church level. Doug is president of *HisChurchatWork.org*, and is one of the early pioneers in implementing workplace ministry in the local church.

Pete Hammond is considered one of the fathers of the modern-day workplace movement and directs the workplace ministry of InterVarsity Christian Fellowship. He has provided a thoughtful "10 Ways" piece that provides great ideas for the local church.

Eric Swanson has contributed to this book by allowing me to include his incredible article, "Ten Paradigm Shifts Toward Community Transformation." Eric writes to the local church about the need for paradigm shifts in how to "do church." I believe this article is an excellent companion to what God is doing in the faith at work movement.

Finally, I wish to thank Dr. Peter Wagner for his contribution of the workplace book bibliography summary and review. Peter has become a good friend and a new voice in this important movement in the body of Christ.

–Os Hillman

How would you like to be the instrument to apply the 80/20 rule to the church today—and move from 20 percent of the people being actively involved in ministry to 80 percent?

How would you like to see your people

▲ experience Christ where they spend 60 to 70 percent of their time?

▲ give more time and money to the work of God?

▲ used as instruments to help transform their families, their workplaces, and your city for Jesus Christ?

Before I get more specific, let me ask another question. Where do a *majority* of men and women spend a *majority* of their time interacting with a *majority* of the lost world? In their neighborhoods? In the local church? No, they spend 60 to 70 percent of their waking hours in the workplace.[1]

We have heard a lot about the 10/40 window of unreached people groups—people who have never heard the gospel. However, the "9 to 5 window" also has a large number of unreached people who have the power to impact the entire world for Jesus Christ once they make a commitment to Him and begin to walk in their destiny. Additionally, there are a large number of Christians in this 9 to 5 window who do not understand their high calling and ministry in and through their work life.

This book is designed to help you see the tremendous opportunity you have as a pastor or church leader to awaken a sleeping giant in the body of Christ—the church in the workplace. For many centuries they have remained quiet and have felt neglected. They do not know exactly what their role is in the body of Christ, but they are asking. They want to be better equipped to serve in the army of the Lord Jesus Christ.

God is marshalling His people in the workplace as never before in history. God is up to something. The next spiritual awakening could take place in the marketplace.

–Henry Blackaby

We hope *The Faith@Work Movement* will be a useful tool for you as a pastor or church leader. There is a fresh Holy Spirit wind blowing through the body of Christ today that could impact the Church as greatly as the early reformation did. We hope this book will increase your awareness and understanding of the current "workplace movement" or "faith at work movement"as many call it today. We have tried to provide you with many practical suggestions on how to plug into what God is doing today in this vital area and tremendously impact your congregation.

Fortune Magazine spoke of the "counterculture bubbling up all over corporate America ... getting organized and going public to agitate for change." God bless you as you seek to learn what it means to equip and release your "agitators for change" in the 9 to 5 Window!

BACKGROUND OF THE WORKPLACE MINISTRY MOVEMENT

The faith at work movement has its early beginnings in the 1950s when the Full Gospel Businessmen's Fellowship International was birthed through Demos Shakarian. This was a group of enthusiastic and passionate businessmen birthed from the Charismatic renewal movement in the '50s and '60s. They now operate in 131 countries. ▶

In 1930 CBMC (Connecting Businessmen to Christ), a non-charismatic marketplace ministry was birthed and continues today with a focus on evangelism to men in the marketplace. These two organizations represent the focus of workplace ministry over the last fifty years. That focus has largely been on executives, men, and evangelism. These ministries were also birthed outside the local church and have often been seen by church leaders as competition to the local church. Many ministries like these have been started because the local church has not understood or embraced their people's passion to reflect their faith in the marketplace.

In the last twelve years there is a new paradigm in workplace ministry unfolding. Twelve years ago we could identify only twenty-five formalized workplace ministries. Today, we have identified twelve hundred organizations that seek to integrate faith and work. These include non-profit workplace ministries, educational institutions, business organizations, and churches that intentionally focus on faith and work. This incredible rate of growth is why many are saying that there is a genuine move of God taking place in this arena that has the potential for changing the spiritual landscape in the local church and cities and nations.

NOT JUST AN EVANGELISM MOVEMENT OUTSIDE THE LOCAL CHURCH

One of the key differences in the modern-day movement is that the focus is no longer evangelism to male executives. The modern-day movement is focused on a more holistic approach to applying faith in the realm where so many people spend so much of their time—their work life. These include students, housewives, those in the military, executives, nurses, doctors, lawyers, and people in entertainment and government. Ministries are no longer just birthing outside the local church as para-church ministries, but local churches are now recognizing the need to equip their people and release them into their workplaces as extended missions of their churches.

There is a trumpet call to return to the early church model of biblical ministry that resides with every believer. This call is to the "9 to 5 Window" where there are more unreached people residing than in the 10/40 window. It is a movement that is designed to change the 80/20 rule in the local church—from 20 percent of people doing ministry to 80 percent. And most of all, it is a movement that is designed to ignite transformation in lives, churches, cities, and nations. Many believe it may be how the Lord will bring genuine revival into our nations because those in the workplace often reside in the place of authority in our cities and have the ability to make significant changes in the way things are done.

If there was ever a time we needed a *tipping point*, it is now. The faith at work movement has the potential to tip the scale from a nation that is falling away from their spiritual roots to a nation that returns to their spiritual destiny. Today, less than 7 percent of people in England attend church. Unless there is a tipping point toward God, America will be following close behind and giving up more ground to ungodly influences that will lead to the demise of our nation.

"… a mostly unorganized mass of believers—a counterculture bubbling up all over corporate America—who want to bridge the traditional divide between spirituality and work. Historically, such folk operated below the radar, on their own or in small workplace groups where they prayed or studied the Bible. But now they are getting organized and going public to agitate for change."

–*Fortune Magazine*, 2001 July 16

Chapter One

A GENUINE
MOVE OF GOD
IS TAKING PLACE IN
THE WORKPLACE

THE MEDIA

In November 1999, *Business Week* magazine noted that "five years ago, only one conference on spirituality and the workplace could be identified; now there are hundreds. There are more than 10,000 Bible and prayer groups in workplaces that meet regularly."

Two years later, *Fortune* magazine affirmed the existence of a movement in a cover story called "God & Business," reporting the marketplace presence of "a mostly unorganized mass of believers —a counterculture bubbling up all over corporate America—who want to bridge the traditional divide between spirituality and work."

The article went on to say:

Historically, such folk operated below the radar, on their own or in small workplace groups where they prayed or studied the Bible. But now they are getting organized and going public to agitate for change. People who want to mix God and business are rebels on several fronts. They reject the centuries-old American conviction that spirituality is a private matter. They challenge religious thinkers who disdain business as an inherently impure pursuit. They disagree with business people who say that religion is unavoidably divisive.

5

In the wake of these articles, the Christian media has also high-lighted the faith at work movement, with stories appearing in *New Man Magazine, Charisma, Christianity Today*, and *Decision* magazines.

CHRISTIAN LEADERS

> I believe
> one of the
> next great
> moves of God
> is going to be
> through the
> believers in the
> workplace.
>
> BILLY GRAHAM

Christian leaders, too, are acknowledging the trend. "I believe one of the next great moves of God is going to be through the believers in the workplace," said Billy Graham. His son, Franklin, put it in the present tense: "God has begun an evangelism movement in the workplace that has the potential to transform our society as we know it."

Kent Humphreys, a businessman and the president of Fellowship of Companies for Christ, a ministry devoted to serving executives and CEOs, wholeheartedly agrees with such assessments: "Leaders in the workplace from every part of the country are experiencing a hunger to be involved and they're searching the web to find those who are of like heart. Those who are a little further along in the movement understand the principle, but are now more anxious for training and practical helps of what it looks like in their workplace."

And the movement is not just an American phenomenon. Brenda de Charmoy, a business consultant from South Africa, remarked: "I am beginning to see more and more people and churches becoming aware that the workplace is a key area for God and we should give it more attention. I think the tide has built quite a lot this last year. There is more questioning by workplace people of the issue of God in their 9 to 5 time. I also see more leaders realizing that going to church and leaving God behind does not work in the end."

Certainly, it does not, and people in myriad places are appreciating that daily. In 1997 I began writing the daily e-mail devotional *TGIF, Today God Is First* (www.freetgifsubscription.net). It has now grown to several hundreds of thousands of readers worldwide. I have learned from the feedback that people are hungry to know how to effectively integrate their faith life with their work life, and they are energized by the call. One subscriber summed it up well: "I never really considered my secular work as a ministry until I read your [devotional]—Now I feel I have as much a ministry as my pastor. I simply have a different mission field."

Let's look more closely at that mission field, that "9 to 5 Window." In several strategic ways, that window is opening wider every day.

> Spirituality
> in the workplace
> is exploding.
>
> –LAURA NASH
> BUSINESS ETHICIST
> HARVARD UNIVERSITY

Larry Julian, business consultant and author of *God Is My CEO* (which has sold more than seventy thousand copies), said he has found an incredible receptivity in secular corporations. "I am seeking more ways to bring my Christian faith into the corporate world where I have spent much of my life. There is an openness that has not been there before."

That openness is partially evidenced by the number of Christian affinity groups that have been birthed within the past decade. The Coca-Cola Christian Fellowship was formed in 2001. Two hundred and seventy-five people attended the first meeting at their world headquarters in Atlanta. Across town, at the Centers for Disease Control (CDC), Angie Tracey launched the first government-approved Christian association—the CDC Christian Fellowship Group. Similar groups have been established at American Airlines, Intel, Texas Instruments, and Sears. In fact, the Christian fellowship at Sears even has its own choir and has produced a professionally recorded CD, underwritten by the company.

THE MOVEMENT IN MAJOR COMPANIES

THE MOVEMENT IN ACADEMIA

Whereas Christian colleges once focused primarily on liberal arts education, today there are almost one hundred business programs in Bible-believing colleges around the world, teaching the next generation of business leaders what it means to lead and manage from a Christian perspective. The Christian Business Faculty Association has grown from its humble beginnings in 1980 to more than four hundred members and its own academic journal, the *Journal of Biblical Integration in Business*.

The academic movement is not limited to Christian schools. InterVarsity Christian Fellowship (IVCF) has launched and/or supported Christian fellowships in dozens of the best secular business schools in the world, including Harvard, Duke, Columbia, Dartmouth, MIT, Michigan, Northwestern, Chicago, Wharton, Virginia, Yale, and the London School of Business.

THE MOVEMENT IN PUBLISHING

Whenever there is a move of God, people write about it. The faith at work movement is no different. In 2000, Pete Hammond, an executive with InterVarsity Press, identified seventy-nine books in the faith at work category. However, in 2002, approximately two dozen books a month were being published in this category, some focusing on leadership and management, others speaking to issues faced by Christian workers generally.

In recent years, magazines such as *Life@Work, The Christian Businessman, Business Reform*, and the *Regent Business Review* have been published for Christians who want to understand more about the faith at work movement.

THE MOVEMENT IN MINISTRIES

The International Coalition of Workplace Ministries (ICWM) and Scruples.net are two ministries that both serve the movement and track its growth. "Ten years ago, we could identify only twenty-five national or international non-profit workplace ministries; today we can identify more than nine hundred," said Mike McLoughlin with YWAM Marketplace Mission. The *International Faith and Work Directory* now features more than twelve hundred listings of ministries, churches, and businesses that have a focus on integrating faith and work. You can access this directory on-line or purchase a copy at *www.icwm.net*.

Among these ministries, some of the larger ones are the Christian Business Men's Committee (ww.cbmc.com), the International Christian Chamber of Commerce (www.iccc.net), the Fellowship of Companies for Christ International (www.fcci.org), the C12 Group (www.theC12group.com), and the Christian Management Association (www.cmaonline.org). Growth in CMA is indicative of the experience of many of these ministries, accelerating from a handful of members in 1976 to over thirty-five hundred CEOs, business owners, middle managers, pastors, and church administrators representing more than fifteen hundred organizations.

Whereas these larger ministries seek to provide full-service training and fellowship to members, many other faith at work ministries are primarily event-driven, usually offering prayer breakfasts or a speaker series. Typical is Bill Leonard, a real estate executive in Atlanta, who decided to reach out to the hi-tech community by sponsoring a once-a-year "High Tech Prayer Breakfast" in Atlanta (www.hightechministries.org). Every October, leaders in the high-tech community come to hear an inspirational talk that usually has a salvation message integrated into it. Table sponsors bring business associates as a means of introducing them to Christ. More than two thousand were in attendance this year.

God has begun an evangelism movement in the workplace that has the potential to transform our society as we know it.

FRANKLIN GRAHAM

THE MOVEMENT IN THE LOCAL CHURCH

George Barna, in his book, *Boiling Point*, said: "Workplace ministry will be one of the core future innovations in church ministry."

He made this assessment several years ago and it is now just beginning to be realized. Doug Sherman, author of *Your Work Matters to God*, cautioned that the local church has been slow to embrace this message.

We should begin to see some changes. Doug Spada's California-based His Church at Work ministry is one of the pioneering efforts to equip the local church to focus on faith at work issues. Spada's ministry does this by creating the infrastructure for a sustainable work-life ministry. His ultimate vision is that churches will send out members to minister in the workplace, just as missionaries are sent out to foreign lands. "We help people launch full-blown ministries within their church," Spada explained. "This isn't, 'Hey, let's meet for breakfast.' This is more of an embedded ministry, just like a men's ministry or a women's ministry or a youth ministry."

Spada added that spiritual renewal movements, particularly in Western culture, are almost always birthed and driven by the less successful, less affluent segments of a society. Karen Jones, director of workplace ministry at Southeast Christian Church in Louisville, Kentucky, agreed: "I believe it is a move of God. I believe it's cutting edge—the next mission field."

This year, Southeast will launch its ministry, which is based on the *HisChurchatWork.org* model. Jones said her early goal is to involve at least half of Southeast's members. With twenty thousand members, the impact in the community could be huge. "Statistics say each person has a sphere of influence of about twenty-five people," Jones commented. "So we could be influencing people—through 250,000 touches a week very quickly."

The five-thousand-member Wooddale Church in Eden Prairie, Minnesota, is another church that has adopted Spada's process. Geoff Bohleen, outreach pastor for Wooddale, says workplace ministry allows his church to reach out to people they never would reach otherwise. "There's no way our pastoral staff is going to get into all those offices, but our people do," he said. "Our pastoral staff is so limited in terms of the connections, the relationships and the friendships we can have with people who need Christ. However, we've got 'Wooddalers' all over the place."

"There is truly no division between sacred and secular except what we have created," said Dallas Willard in *The Spirit of the Disciplines*. "And that is why the division of the legitimate roles and functions of human life into the sacred and secular does incalculable damage to our individual lives and the cause of Christ. Holy people must stop going into 'church work' as their natural course of action and take up holy orders in farming, industry, law, education, banking, and journalism with the same zeal previously given to evangelism or to pastoral and missionary work."

That message is getting through, as the faith at work movement sweeps across the land. And the potential is great for it to effect genuine revival across the culture.

Peter Wagner, noted church growth expert and former professor at Fuller Theological Seminary, foresees this revival, too:

> "I believe the workplace movement has the potential to impact society as much as the reformation did. I have read sixty-four books on this movement and have fifty-four pages of handwritten notes. It is what the Spirit is saying to the churches today."

A CATALYST FOR REVIVAL

In the last twelve to twenty-four months I have personally noticed a surge of interest. I see an openness from pastors that is very new that I have not seen before. I see a Kingdom mentality. I promise you we are within months of a major move of God.

–KENT HUMPRHEYS
PRESIDENT, FCCI

New Ventures, a division of the Billy Graham Evangelistic Association (BGEA), was established to identify trends in the body of Christ and to determine where they will invest their ministry resources in the future. They first looked at fifty-two different categories of ministry and then narrowed it down twenty-eight then twelve. Eventually, they narrowed the list to four, with the workplace movement as one of the three areas where they are now focused because they believe this is one of the primary areas where God is moving at the present time.

In the spring of 2003, New Ventures teamed with an organization I lead, the International Coalition of Workplace Ministries (ICWM), to host a workplace conference at The Cove in Asheville, North Carolina. More than 270 workplace leaders, workplace ministries' representatives, and pastors were in attendance. New Ventures has decided to host regional events around the country on this topic.

There is a revival coming that is returning us to our roots to understand what the early church understood: work is a holy calling in which God moves to transform lives, cities, and nations.

"Someone recently said that the 'First' Reformation took the Word of God to the common man and woman; the 'Second' Reformation is taking the *work* of God to the common man and woman," noted Tom Phillips, vice president of training for the BGEA, in a message to conference attendees at The Cove Conference Center. "That time is now. The greatest potential ministry in the world today is the marketplace. Christ's greatest labor force is those men and women already in that environment."

Indeed, we live in historic times. Using the collective hands in companies, ministries, colleges, the media, and the local church, God has suddenly and providentially created a 9 to 5 Window.[1]

Is there any precedent to this modern-day move of God in the workplace? Yes, Jesus set the best example of this. Let's look at His life in regard to how He ministered in the workplace.

Someone recently said that the 'First' Reformation took the Word of God to the common man and woman; the 'Second' Reformation is taking the *work* of God to the common man and woman. That time is now. The greatest potential ministry in the world today is the marketplace. Christ's greatest labor force is those men and women already in that environment.

–Tom Phillips
vice president of training
Billy Graham
Evangelistic Association

THE WORKPLACE MINISTRY OF JESUS AND TODAY'S GREAT DIVIDE

Have you ever considered that Jesus modeled workplace ministry? It is easy to forget that Jesus spent more than 50 percent of His adult life in a carpentry shop. He was more known for being a carpenter than He was for being the Son of God. Perhaps that is why so many people had difficulty reconciling Jesus, the carpenter, with Jesus the Son of God who did miracles in the workplace. Consider the following amazing facts:

▲ The New Testament records that Jesus appeared publicly 132 times—122 were in the marketplace.

▲ Jesus told 52 parables—45 had a workplace context.

▲ Acts recorded 40 divine interventions—39 were in the marketplace.

▲ Jesus spent His adult life as a carpenter until the age of thirty when He began a public preaching ministry in the workplace.

▲ Jesus called 12 workplace individuals—not clergy— to build His Church.

▲ Work is *worship*. The Hebrew word *avodah* is the root word for both *work* and *worship*.

▲ Work in its different forms is mentioned more than 800 times in the Bible—more than all the words used to express *worship, music, praise,* and *singing* combined.

15

His doing nothing wonderful
(his first 30 years)
is in itself a kind of wonder.
—Saint Bonaventure

◆

Preach the gospel always,
and when necessary, use words.
—St. Francis of Assisi

▲ "54 percent of Jesus' reported teaching ministry arose out of issues posed by others in the scope of daily life experience." –Lewis and Lewis, LICC

Yes, Jesus was a workplace minister who combined both a priestly call with a workplace call. In the mind of Jesus, there was no sacred/secular divide. He did not consider His work life to be less important than His spiritual life. Both were entwined in everyday life. The Hebrews understood this. There was not a separation of the *faith life* from the *work life*.

Oswald Chambers, well-known author of *My Utmost for His Highest*, said: "The spiritual manifests itself in a life which knows no division into sacred and secular."

THE GREAT DIVIDE: ELEVATING THE SPIRITUAL AT THE EXPENSE OF THE SECULAR

If you were to conduct a survey on an average city street and ask if religion belonged in the workplace, chances are high that most answers would be no, and that would be correct. *Religion* doesn't, but *Jesus* does. Most people today, even many Christians, see no relevance between God and work in today's fast-paced society. Why is this? It goes back to the early years before the protestant reformation. Consider the following history from Os Guinness's book, *The Call*, of this segmented worldview:

> The truth of calling means that for followers of Christ, "everyone, everywhere, and in everything" lives the whole of life as a response to God's call. Yet, this holistic character of calling has often been distorted to become a form of dualism that elevates the spiritual at the expense of the secular. This distortion may be called the "Catholic distortion" because it rose in the Catholic era and is the majority position in the Catholic tradition. Protestants, however, cannot afford to be

smug. *For one thing, countless Protestants have succumbed to the Catholic distortion as William Wilberforce nearly did (he almost went into the "ministry" after salvation but was counseled to stay in politics). Ponder for example, the fallacy of the contemporary Protestant term "full-time Christian service"—as if those not working for churches or Christian organizations are only part-time in the service of Christ. For another thing, Protestant confusion about calling has led to a "Protestant distortion" that is even worse. This is a form of dualism in a secular direction that not only elevates the secular at the expense of the spiritual, but also cuts it off from the spiritual altogether.*[1]

It is understandable why we are where we are today. Throughout centuries, we have been trained to believe that the two worlds of spiritual and secular are to be separated.

> Workplace ministry is an intentional focus of equipping men and women in all spheres of work and society to understand and experience their work and life as a holy calling from God.
>
> –Os HILLMAN

"FULL-TIME" VERSUS "PART-TIME" CHRISTIANS

May the favor of the Lord our God rest upon us; establish the work of our hands for us—yes, establish the work of our hands. (Ps. 90:17 NIV)

Throughout the church, a view of those in "full-time" Christian work versus those who work "secular" jobs has created a definite class distinction. There seems to be little evidence of this distinction in the Bible. Yet, we often hear testimonies from those who left "regular" jobs to go into the mission field, or some other "full-time" Christian work.

My good friend, Rich Marshall, has been a pastor for more than thirty years. Rich came to the realization of this great divide. He recognized the calling that members of his congregation had to the workplace, so he began ordaining them for this call. He

> *It is an error to think that those who flee worldly affairs and engage in contemplation are leading an angelic life... We know that men were created to busy themselves with labor and that no sacrifice is more pleasing to God than when each one attends to his calling and studies well to live for the common good.*
>
> *—John Calvin*

realized that so often his fellow ministers had been guilty of training those in the marketplace to do the *church's* ministry instead of *their own* ministry. These are not necessarily the same, nor do they require the same skills. In his book, *God@Work*, Rich wrote the following regarding *clergy* and *laity*:

> *Two little words, words that misrepresent God and His plan, have been used by the enemy to bring about the development of a caste system within the Body of Christ—those who are called to professional ministry or full-time ministry: the "clergy," and those who are not: the "laity." It is my conviction that all of us in the Body of Christ are called to full-time ministry. When we allow this caste system to disturb our thinking, we create a problem for many who experience the strong call of God on their lives. We need both a terminology and a mind-set that works to eliminate the second-class citizen concept in the Kingdom of God.[2]*

John Beckett is a business leader who has written an excellent book for business leaders—*Loving Monday*. He related his own journey into understanding the call of God. He wrote:

> *For years, I thought my involvement in business was a second-class endeavor—necessary to put bread on the table, but somehow less noble than the more sacred pursuits, like being a minister or a missionary. The clear impression was that to truly serve God, one must leave business and go into "full-time Christian service." I have met countless other businesspeople who feel the same way.[3]*

A surprisingly large number of pastors subscribe to my *TGIF*

(*Today God Is First*) Internet devotional that I write for men and women in the workplace. One day I received a very simple note from a pastor that said: "How can a businessman have such wisdom?" This question spoke volumes to me. Basically, it seemed to imply that clergy are the only ones in tune with the spiritual matters of life—workplace believers focus on the "secular" life. However, God has never said this. He is helping many of us begin to understand our true calling as disciples of the Lord Jesus, but with different roles to play in the body of Christ—and no role is less "holy" than another. I realize this could challenge some church leaders because there is an implied "higher calling" premise when one responds to a call of vocational ministry.

There is an unspoken spiritual hierarchy in our society that seems to place spiritual calling and value based on vocational position. It goes something like this:

- ▲ pastor
- ▲ missionary
- ▲ evangelist
- ▲ church worker
- ▲ vocational ministry worker
- ▲ stay-at-home mom
- ▲ plumber
- ▲ CEO/executive
- ▲ ad agency executive (scum of the earth!)

Mark Greene, director of the London Institute for Contemporary Christianity, shared a similar concept at one of our annual International Coalition of Workplace Ministries gatherings. Mark and I both come from an ad agency background, so we can poke fun at our former profession. However, seriously

The most common self-inflicted put-down is "I am not a pastor—I am just a layperson." This is all part of a clever satanic scheme to neutralize apostles, prophets, evangelists, pastors and teachers along with the entire army of disciples, already positioned in the marketplace.

—ED SILVOSO
ANOINTED FOR BUSINESS
HARVEST EVANGELISM

speaking, God has never said that one profession has more spiritual value than another. We all have different roles and callings. Just as Jesus had a work to do before His Father, we each are called to a specific work for which we will be judged and rewarded.

We should not consider this as a lessening of the call of vocational ministry but to realize our strategic role as equippers of workplace believers who have the potential to transform families, workplaces, cities, and nations. Church leaders have a tremendous opportunity to impact society through working people.

When I received Christ in 1974, I was a professional golfer. God gradually led me away from golf and into business. In 1980, I considered moving into "full-time" Christian work by attending a short-term Bible school to determine if I wanted to be a pastor. I served briefly as an assistant pastor only to have the position removed. It was never God's intention for me to be a pastor.

Implied guilt rather than a genuine call of God led me to consider "vocational ministry." I believed I might not be giving my all to God if I wasn't in "full-time Christian ministry." I have learned since then that *work* truly is *worship* to God. If you are in a secular job that doesn't violate Scripture, your vocation is just as important to God as full-time missionary work in India. God calls each of us to a vocation. He desires to use us for His Kingdom in that vocation.

In their book, *Your Work Matters to God*, Doug Sherman and William Hendricks stated the following regarding holy versus unholy vocations:

> *The architect who designs buildings to the glory of God,*
> *who works with integrity, diligence, fairness, and excellence,*
> *who treats his wife with the love Christ has for the Church,*

> Much of our culture has a distinctly Greek view of work: We work out of necessity. But, you see, we are made in the image of God, and as such we are made to work—to create, to shape, to bring order out of disorder.
>
> –Chuck Colson[4]

who raises his children in Godly wisdom and instruction,
who urges non-Christian coworkers and associates to heed
the gospel message—in short, who acts as a responsible
manager in the various arenas God has entrusted him—
this man will receive eternal praise from God. That is
what really matters in eternity. In short, God's interest is
not simply that we do holy activities but that we become
holy people. Not pious. Not sanctimonious. Not other-
worldly. But pure, healthy, Christlike.

This whole idea of secular versus religious is a Greek
idea. These Greek ideas, clothed in biblical language, have
for the most part, been passed down unchallenged to suc-
ceeding generations of Christians. As a result, most of us
today bring assumptions to the biblical text, assumptions
based on a worldview articulated by Plato, Aristotle,
Plotinus, and other Greek thinkers. Likewise, if you have
been around much Christian teaching, you've undoubtedly
been influenced by at least some Greek ideas. Nothing
overtly or purely pagan. But I suggest that Christianity in
our culture has absorbed from its tradition a number of
subtle beliefs that trace back to Greek philosophy. Now I am
not "down" on philosophy. Nor am I "down" on the Greek
philosophers, for they have provided us with many insights
into philosophical questions. Nevertheless, reading the Bible
through their eyes—through Greek glasses—can severely
distort the truth of God's Word. We will think that the Bible
says things it does not say, and overlook important things it
does say. The result will be a distorted view of life. And a
distorted view of work. Wearing Greek glasses, one would
tend to ignore or disparage everyday work. This is how
work looks when viewed through these lenses.[5]

Greek Influence

Sherman makes an excellent assessment here of how many Western societies have been affected by the philosophies and culture of the Greek influence. We may speak English, but we think "Greek." Our focus on competition, segmentation of life from the secular to sacred, rationalism and reasoning—all move us to a more intellectual position in our faith rather than to a simple, trusting faith. The Greek/Hellenistic civilization has been so much a part of our thinking and way of viewing life that we have lost our ability to understand God and relate to Him as the early Church did.

As the Church grew and extended its borders outside Jerusalem, believers became influenced by a wide array of philosophies. The purity and power of the gospel message were affected by the dominant Greek culture. Following the two major Jewish revolts of A.D. 70 and A.D. 135, a Greek, man-centered view of the world reshaped the Church. Early Greek scholars like Plato introduced dualism, which says that life is divided into two compartments: the spiritual or eternal, and the temporal realm of the physical. Plato's dualism entered the Church through many of the Church fathers that were Greek philosophers who had converted to Christianity. They attempted to reconcile Greek thought with Christianity.

Following is a comparison of the Hebraic model and the Greek model of ministry within a local church, developed by Mike and Sue Dowgiewicz, authors of *Restoring the Early Church*, a book on comparing the early Church to our modern-day, Greek-influenced Church.

HEBRAIC	GREEK
Active—appeals to the heart	Cognitive—appeals to the intellect
Process Oriented	**_Program Oriented_**
• Emphasizes direct participation	• Heavy program emphasis
• Emphasizes age and wisdom	• Emphasizes education
• Role modeling, mentoring, and discipleship indispensable	• Relies on speaking skills, oratory, programmed materials, information conveyance
• Leadership by personal example	• Leader's personal life less essential
• Character of leaders essential	
• Personal relationships essential	• Personal relationships optional
Biblical Application	**_Biblical Application_**
• Doers of the Word	• Belief without cost to self
• Bible—reality that must be confronted	• Bible—data that must be taught
• Goal—develop Christlikeness	• Focus on rules—dos and don'ts
	• Emphasizes distinct denominations
Ministry Activity	**_Ministry Activity_**
• Small intimate groups	• Large impersonal groups
• Leader as facilitator	• Leader-directed and controlled
• Cooperative, participatory planning	• Organizational roles important
• Spiritual gifts shared	• Acquisition of knowledge emphasized
• Frequent scheduled and unscheduled gatherings	• Reliance on scheduled gatherings
Fruit	**_Fruit_**
• Love, acceptance, forgiveness	• Mutual toleration
• Transparency encouraged	• Transparency discouraged
• Active participation	• Passivity and lethargy
• "How you serve" vital	• "What you know" vital
• Each believer trained to serve	• Trained professionals utilized
• Produces mature believers	• Produces spectators

Source: *Restoring the Early Church*, Mike and Sue Dowgiewicz, Aslan Group Publishing

The Value of Secular Work

In the *Word in Life Study Bible*, Pete Hammond provides some good insights into God's view of this great divide—secular versus sacred work. God values our work even when the product has no eternal value. Christians often measure the significance of a job by its perceived value from the eternal perspective. Will the work last; will it "really count" for eternity? The implication is that God approves of work for eternity, but places little value on work for the here and now. By this measure, the work of ministers and missionaries has eternal value because it deals with people's spiritual, eternal needs. By contrast, the work of a salesman, teller, or typist has only limited value, because it meets only earthly needs. In other words, this kind of work doesn't really "count" in God's eyes. But this way of thinking overlooks several important truths.

1 God Himself has created a world that is time-bound and temporary (2 Peter 3:10,11). Yet He values His work, declaring it to be "very good," by its very nature (Gen. 1:31; Acts 14:17).

2 God promises rewards to people in everyday jobs, based on their attitude and conduct (Eph. 6:8; Col. 3:23-4:1).

3 God cares about the everyday needs of people as well as their spiritual needs. He cares whether people have food, clothing, and shelter.

4 God cares about people who will enter eternity. To the extent that a job serves the needs of people, God values it, because He values people.[6]

Skillful Work Is a Ministry unto the Lord

Do you see a man skilled in his work? He will serve before kings; he will not serve before obscure men (Prov. 22:29 NIV).

The Lord has called each of us to be excellent in what we do. Those whom God used in the Kingdom as workplace ministers were skilled and exemplified excellence in their fields. Not only were these men skilled, they were filled with God's Spirit. Then the Lord said to Moses, *"See, I have chosen Bezalel son of Uri, the son of Hur, of the tribe of Judah, and I have filled him with the Spirit of God, with skill, ability and knowledge in all kinds of crafts—to make artistic designs for work in gold, silver and bronze, to cut and set stones, to work in wood, and to engage in all kinds of craftsmanship"* (Ex. 31:1-5).

Consider Huram, the master craftsman of bronze to whom Solomon entrusted much of the temple designs. He was a true master craftsman (see 1 Kings 7:14). Consider Joseph, whose skill as an administrator was known throughout Egypt and the world. Consider Daniel, who served his king with great skill and integrity. The list could go on—David (soldier and king), Nehemiah (government worker), Aquila and Priscilla (tentmakers). Most of these were in the "secular" world of work providing a needed service.

It is important for church leaders to help break down this wall of separation. Your people need to know they have a workplace calling that is as important as your calling to a vocational ministry. They need to be affirmed and valued as ministers in their spheres of influence. They need to feel they are not "second-class citizens." It is time to affirm the workers in your congregation as men and women on a mission from God, in their workplaces where they spend 60 to 70 percent of their time. Whatever you do, work at it with all your heart, as working for the Lord, not for men, since you know that you will receive an inheritance from the Lord as a reward. It is the Lord Christ you are serving.[7]

INDICATORS OF A PROBLEM

Chapter Three

Dear Brother Os:

I have been the secretary for Judson Cornwall, Bible teacher and author of 53 books, for 13 years. Judson is 76, suffering from diabetes, and he is slowly cutting down his once hectic schedule. I have felt the Lord directing me into another line of work to prepare me for the time when Judson retires. I love computers. I love to teach others about computers and I very much enjoy repairing them. Recently at the age of 55, I went to school so I could become a certified computer tech, but then guilt came upon me. Why would the Lord allow me to follow such a course of work as this? It isn't a very "Christian" field to be in. I told myself that surely the Lord needs computer people, too. I help a lot of my Christian friends with their computers, don't I (for no charge)? Then someone sent an e-mail to Judson with your article, "The Fallacy of Full-time Christian Work." It was talking to me and set my mind at ease about being in the computer field. We are all on the mission field—wherever our calling is—and the Lord will use us as we are willing to be used. Thank you for giving me this little shove that I so desperately needed. I have plans and ideas for what I want to accomplish and I will count on God's grace and guidance to help me. May He richly bless you in this new year before us,

> *Terri Gargis*
> *Glendale, AZ*

Let me share some alarming statistics with you that reveal the depth of the problem we have among general workers in society. This foundational problem is at the core of why we need to address this area of faith at work.

A San Francisco radio station survey revealed an amazing 80 percent dissatisfaction rate among the general population as it relates to their work life. *The Wall Street Journal* confirmed the same 80 percent dissatisfaction rate among general workers in their surveys and found a 50 percent dissatisfaction rate among executives. And five hundred surveys conducted by Doug Sherman, author of *Your Work Matters to God*, discovered that even among Christians there is a 50 percent dissatisfaction rate with their jobs.[1]

These numbers tell us that we have a crisis among people—nonbelievers and believers—when it comes to finding meaning and purpose in their vocations. They tell us we have a society that is simply collecting a check every week and seeing no spiritual value in the daily work life experience. This fact results in a great deal of job disloyalty, job change, and poor job performance. As for the Christian workers, it means they definitely do not see their work as a ministry or a place where they are experiencing the love and power of Christ. They check their faith at the door on Monday morning and believe that is what everyone else does instead of recognizing one of the greatest mission fields on earth.

Either these are not the gospels, or we're not Christians.

–THOMAS LINACRE, Henry VIII's doctor and Renaissance thinker after he was given the four gospels in Greek.
(Five years later Martin Luther hammered some church theses to a church door, and the Protestant Reformation began.)

THE LACK OF ETHICS IN THE WORKPLACE TODAY

Sales and Marketing magazine conducted a survey in 2001 that revealed the ethics currently modeled in the general workplace. Here are some of the results:

▲ Cheating on an expense report—58 percent
▲ Working a second job on company time—50 percent
▲ Rushing closed deals through accounting before they were really closed—36 percent
▲ Listing a "strip bar" as a restaurant on an expense report —22 percent
▲ Giving a kickback to a customer—19 percent [2]

It is no wonder we have an ethics crisis within corporate America. This alone should dispel any doubt of the impelling need to bring the gospel into the workplace.

NO SIGNIFICANT DIFFERENCE IN THE ETHICS OF THE CHURCH AND THE UNCHURCHED

In December 1983, The Princeton Religion Research Center published a landmark survey conducted for *The Wall Street Journal* by the Gallup Organization. The researchers measured a wide range of moral and ethical behaviors, such as calling in sick when not sick, cheating on income tax, and pilfering company supplies for personal use. The results were disappointing, to say the least.

But what the researchers found most startling was *that there was no significant difference between the churched and the unchurched in their ethics and values on the job.* In other words, despite the fact that more and more people attend churches, churches seem to be having less and less of an impact on the moral fiber of their people, at least in the workplace.

To quote the researchers: "These findings ... will come as a shock to the religious leaders and underscore the need for religious leaders to channel the new religious interest in America not simply into religious involvement but in deep spiritual commitment."[3]

Lack of Training

Doug Sherman said, "Our surveys reveal that 90 to 97 percent of Christians have never heard a sermon relating biblical principles to their work life."[4] When I first read this statistic I questioned the accuracy of such an alarming figure. I had heard others use figures in the 40 to 50 percent range for this trend. However, in my own random surveys among people and groups, I have asked this question: How many of you have been intentionally trained at church to apply biblical faith in your work life? That means you have been in a Bible study, heard a sermon series, or had a training course on applying biblical faith at work.

The percentage of hands that go up is consistent—3 to 5 percent. So, I believe that Sherman's figure is still accurate.

Further studies have found that 47 percent of people surveyed say that the preaching and teaching they receive is irrelevant to their daily lives.[5] Given these statistics, it is no wonder the average Christian has had no spiritual impact on their workplace and has been unable to integrate their faith life into their work life.

SO WHERE'S THE IMPACT?

What percentage of market share do you think Coca-Cola has in the soft drink industry?

☐ 3% ☐ 10% ☐ 20% ☐ 40% ☐ 50%

The answer is 40 percent. I think you would agree that Coca-Cola has a tremendous impact on the business world and even on society. When Coca-Cola is involved people listen. The company carries a certain level of clout and authority because they have such a high percentage of market share.

As a former ad agency owner, I dealt with market share among companies and products. I often like to view the Church in terms of market share. In other words, how many Christians are there in our society? George Barna has researched this for many years. Over the last ten years he has found that 35 to 45 percent of the general population would describe themselves as "born again Christians" when defined as "one who has placed their faith and trust in the Lord Jesus Christ." The U.S. Bureau of Labor Statistics told us that in 1998 there were 140 million adult workers.[6] That would calculate to approximately 56 million "born again Christian" adult workers in the U.S. based on the comparable ratio from Barna's surveys. If Christians have the same level of market share as Coca-Cola—*where is our impact on the culture and the workplace?*

I think you would agree that either the figures are grossly wrong, or the Church is anemic. I tend to think that the latter is the case. The Church has become like a large luxury ocean liner instead of a battleship designed for spiritual warfare in the place where most of the unsaved congregate—the workplace.

54% of Jesus' reported teaching ministry arose out of issues posed by others in the scope of daily life experience.

–LEWIS AND LEWIS
LONDON INSTITUTE OF
CONTEMPORARY CHRISTIANITY

WORKPLACE MINISTRY IN THE LOCAL CHURCH

In this section we want to address the role of workplace ministry within the context of the local church. I have identified twelve fallacies of belief that hinder the work of God among believers in the workplace that are often held by church leaders. These beliefs must be addressed in order for us to effectively equip and release men and women to fulfill their calling in and through their work life. The local church has the opportunity to be the primary distribution point for equipping and commissioning for ministry in the workplace.

When we begin to view the 9 to 5 Window as a major mission field for the local church, we will begin to see real change take place in our society. However, up until now, we have viewed workplace believers as the source of funding and service for our overseas mission projects and internal ministry activities instead of seeing these people as missionaries that need to be equipped to impact their own workplace mission fields.

TWELVE FALLACIES OF BELIEF OFTEN HELD BY THE CHURCH AND A FIVE-YEAR FORECAST

1. *There is a God-ordained spiritual hierarchy in calling.* Nowhere in Scripture can we say that there is one vocation more holy and spiritual than another. God always deals at the individual level. There are different roles and responsibilities as it relates to leadership, but the calling is equal to any other calling.

> *Whatever you do, work at it with all your heart, as working for the Lord, not for men, since you know that you will receive an inheritance from the Lord as a reward. It is the Lord Christ you are serving* (Col. 3:23-24 NIV).

2. *A workplace believer's primary role is to fund the church's ministry.* Viewing your workplace believers as the primary source to fund the work of ministry is like viewing your spouse only to meet your sexual needs. God has created each person with unique talents and gifts to build the Kingdom of God. Funding the work of ministry is only one role of each member of the body of Christ.

TWELVE FALLACIES OF BELIEF OFTEN HELD BY THE CHURCH

> *There are different kinds of gifts, but the same Spirit.*
> *There are different kinds of service, but the same Lord.*
> *There are different kinds of working, but the same God*
> *works all of them in all men (1 Cor. 12:4-6).*

3. *The profit motive is evil.* When David considered confronting Goliath, he first determined the benefits related to winning the battle in addition to the spiritual nature of the battle. The profit motive was a part of David's decision-making process. The profit motive is necessary in the workplace and believers should be encouraged to understand the balance between the spiritual and the physical in doing business.

> *The king will give great wealth to the man who kills him.*
> *He will also give him his daughter in marriage and will exempt*
> *his father's family from taxes in Israel (1 Sam. 17:26).*

4. *Ministry is primarily what takes place within the four walls of the local church.* The early Church's primary place of ministry was in the place where most of the people met— their workplaces. Of forty miracles in the book of Acts, thirty-nine were in the marketplace.

> *For where two or three come together in my name,*
> *there am I with them (Matt. 18:20).*

> *The apostles performed many miraculous signs*
> *and wonders among the people. And all the believers used*
> *to meet together in Solomon's Colonnade (Acts 5:12).*

5. *Workplace ministry is an evangelism program to executives.* Workplace ministry is an intentional focus of equipping men and women in *all* spheres of work and society to understand and experience their work and life as a holy calling from God. Evangelism is not an end goal of workplace ministry; it is the fruit. It is about experiencing the fullness of God in all aspects of our work life.

> *All things were created through Him and for Him.*
> *And He is before all things, and in Him all things consist*
> (Col. 1:16-17 NKJV).

6. *Five-fold ministry is primarily reserved for those in full-time vocational ministry.* Nowhere does the passage below indicate that this is related only to those in full-time vocational ministry. There was no such thing in the early Church.

> *It was he who gave some to be apostles,*
> *some to be prophets, some to be evangelists, and some to*
> *be pastors and teachers, to prepare God's people for works of*
> *service, so that the body of Christ may be built up until we all*
> *reach unity in the faith and in the knowledge of the Son of*
> *God and become mature, attaining to the whole measure*
> *of the fullness of Christ.* (Eph. 4:11-13)

7. *Planting churches in the workplace will take money and resources away from the local church.* There is no evidence to support this statement. More evidence reveals the exact opposite is true. There are many churches giving a focus to this important area of ministry. As believers feel equipped and released to minister in their mission field, they get more excited about being a vital part of the local body.

> *And my God shall supply all your need according*
> *to His riches in glory by Christ Jesus* (Phil. 4:19 NKJV).

8. ***Workplace ministry is yet another program to be managed by the pastor.*** If workplace ministry is part of the DNA of the church it is not a ministry by itself. It is more an integrated philosophy of ministry. It helps to have a workplace champion to coordinate and give leadership to this important area, but it should not be considered another stand-alone ministry inside the church.

9. ***I am already equipping my people to be effective in their workplace.*** Many pastors genuinely believe they are equipping their people. However, research reveals that 47 percent of people surveyed say that preaching and teaching is irrelevant to their daily lives and 90 to 97 percent say they have never been trained to apply biblical faith in their work life. The key word is *relevant*. Most feel the teaching is not relevant to their specific world. Pastors must learn how to break down teaching to a deeper level of application to workplace situations in order for it to be perceived as relevant to the average workplace believer.

> *I have become all things to all men that I might by all means save some. Now this I do for the gospel's sake, that I may be partaker of it with you* (1 Cor. 9:22-23 NKJV).

10. ***Pastors have the inside track on spiritual truth.*** The New Testament was written by working Christians. Non-vocational ministry people, such as Jeremiah Lanphier in the 1858 revival that began in New York City, have led some of our most important spiritual movements. Pastors are the shepherds and should provide equipping of the saints. However, many workplace believers have strong teaching and equipping gifts as well, they simply get their paychecks from the workplace.

And He Himself gave some to be apostles, some prophets, some
evangelists, and some pastors and teachers, for the equipping
of the saints for the work of ministry (Eph. 4:11 NKJV).

Nowhere does this passage say it is only for vocational ministry workers.

11. **Workplace believers are difficult to motivate in spiritual things because they are consumed with worldly matters.**
Sometimes pastors feel they cannot get their people motivated and involved in the their local church ministry. Many times it is because these people have a ministry in the workplace and sometimes do not feel called to a local church volunteer ministry. We need to help workplace believers understand how to be equipped and released to minister where they are called.

And say to Archippus, "Take heed to the ministry
which you have received in the Lord, that you may fulfill it"
(Col. 4:17 NKJV).

12. **We can do "church" the same way we've always done it. This is just another fad.** God is doing a new thing in the body of Christ today. We must move with the Spirit of God in how He wants his life to be expressed to and through His body. "Even the most committed Christian is only attending church an average of two times a month according to a Gallup poll. It's a lot like preaching to a parade," said Dr. Eddie Gibbs, a Fuller Seminary professor.

… the sons of Issachar who had understanding of the times,
to know what Israel ought to do (1 Chron. 12:32 NKJV).

MUSTARD SEED FAITH IN BUSINESS

He replied, "Because you have so little faith. I tell you the truth, if you have faith as small as a mustard seed, you can say to this mountain, 'Move from here to there' and it will move. Nothing will be impossible for you."

MATTHEW 17:20

Does God do miracles in the workplace? Is He concerned about the mountains we face in our work life? Does He want us to bring the everyday problems we face in the workplace to His attention? The answer to every one of these questions is yes. God wants to be involved in every aspect of our lives.

Gunnar Olson, the Swedish founder of the International Christian Chamber of Commerce, tells a story about God performing a miracle in his own business a few years ago. He owns a plastics company in Sweden; they make huge plastic bags that are used to cover bales of hay in the farmlands across Europe. It was the harvest season and they were getting ready to ship thousands of pallets of these bags to their customers. More than one thousand pallets were ready to ship when an alarming discovery was made. Every bag on the warehouse floor had sealed shut from top to bottom! Scientists declared the entire stock as worthless trash. Nothing could be done. The company would go out of business.

Gunnar, his wife, and children sought the Lord in prayer about this catastrophe. The Holy Spirit spoke through various family members. His wife said, "If God can turn water into wine, what are plastics?"

His daughter said, "I don't believe this is from the Lord. We should stand against it."

Gunnar sensed they were to trust God for a miracle in this situation. They began to pray. They took authority over this "mountain" of a problem—based on Matthew 17, which gave them the authority to cast a mountain into the sea if faith only the size of a mustard seed could be exercised.

The following Monday they went to the warehouse and laid hands on every pallet asking the Lord to restore the bags to their original condition. It took several hours. Later, the employees began to inspect the bags. As they inspected the bags, they discovered that every single bag had been restored to its original condition! An incredible miracle had taken place.

God sets the stage to allow His power to be revealed for those willing to exercise the faith of a mustard seed. All things are possible with God.[1]

Any move of God will be attacked if it threatens Satan's foundations. Satan does not attack a movement in the vision phase. However, when a vision is birthed and it has the potential for threatening a long-held establishment or tradition, you can expect it to be attacked. This attack often comes through the religious establishment—just as Jesus' most ardent enemies were from the religious establishment.

Following is what we can expect to see in the next five years as a result of God's move among believers in the workplace:

▲ *Training in the local church* designed to help men and women conceptualize their work as ministry with practical application.

▲ *Churches viewed as equipping centers* that will support Christians in their workplace calling.

▲ *A movement similar to Promise Keepers,* with major events centered around the faith at work theme.

▲ *The men's movement will integrate this message* into their focus.

▲ *Corporations will begin to take a more proactive acceptance* of faith at work issues.

▲ *Prayer will impact the workplace.*

▲ *Our first cities will transformed* because those in authority become active and passionate about their faith where they work.

▲ *Faith will be openly expressed* in government agencies, the entertainment industries, educational institutions, and corporate workplaces.

▲ *Many people will come to Christ* as more major ministries embrace this move of God and integrate it into their focus.

▲ *Miracles will be experienced in the marketplace* because of "new wineskin" Christians who are willing to move in faith and obedience into arenas the religious leaders have believed heretofore taboo.

▲ *A paradigm shift will take place for many pastors.* The majority of pastors will be the last to embrace the movement, but will ultimately be responsible for the greatest influence once they do embrace it. There will be a few early innovator pastors who will provide leadership to the movement that will allow other pastors to embrace it.

If people try to overly organize around the movement it will be the beginning of the death of it. It cannot become another program. When it becomes a program it loses its power and life. Workplace ministry must become part of the DNA of the local church to have any impact.

WORK IS MINISTRY
WORK TO MINISTER

Chapter Five

WORK IS MINISTRY

Many times I see church leaders define workplace ministry as an evangelism program to the executive. However, when we speak of workplace ministry we are speaking in a broader, more holistic approach to God's view of work. There are two core attributes to seeing work as ministry. Workplace ministry is a broader, more holistic approach to God's view of work than simply an evangelism program targeting executives. Work as ministry has two core attributes.

First, I believe we can say biblically that *work itself can be ministry*. The word *ministry* comes from the word *service*. Service to others is in itself a ministry. Paul said that everything we do is ministry because we are doing it unto the Lord: "Whatever you do, work at it with all your heart, as working for the Lord, not for men, since you know that you will receive an inheritance from the Lord as a reward. It is the Lord Christ you are serving" (Col. 3:23-24).

Second, *work is also worship*. As we discussed earlier, *avodah* is the root word from which we get the words *work* and *worship*. God actually views our work as worship, not as a curse. Eric Liddell, the Olympic gold medal runner who was the star of *Chariots of Fire*, replied remarkably to a challenge from his religious sister. She wanted him to focus on going to the mission field instead of focusing his attention on running. He said, "When I run I feel His pleasure." Eric knew God created him for worship and that worship took many forms. His sister had fallen prey to a religious spirit prevalent in today's Church that deems nonreligious activity as evil and of no spiritual value. However, this is clearly not biblical.

There is value in secular work simply because it meets needs found in society. God created mankind with many different gifts and talents to serve the multifaceted needs of human beings. What a wonderful and creative God we serve!

GOD'S REDEMPTION OF WORK

Cursed is the ground because of you; through painful toil you will eat of it all the days of your life. It will produce thorns and thistles for you, and you will eat the plants of the field. By the sweat of your brow you will eat your food until you return to the ground, since from it you were taken; for dust you are and to dust you will return. (Gen. 3:17-19 NIV)

God redeemed not only man's sin when He went to the cross, but He also redeemed all that was fallen in the Garden of Eden. When Jesus died on the cross, His death was designed to redeem all that was lost—including the curse that was placed upon the ground. Note that what was really cursed was the ground. Because the ground was cursed, work would become more difficult. The work itself was not what was cursed.

Jesus prayed: *"Our Father in heaven, hallowed be your name, your kingdom come, your will be done on earth as it is in heaven"* (Matt. 6:9-10). God wanted to redeem all that was lost by manifesting the Kingdom of God in all aspects of earthly life.

THE ETERNAL SALES CALL

I received a phone call from the technology CEO. It was our second conversation. He had begun receiving my TGIF devotional a few weeks earlier, compliments of his mother-in-law. Each day he read the daily message and found that it really helped him in some of his personal and professional life struggles.

He felt his technology product might have some application to my ministry; I asked about how he started receiving the devotional. As he told me his story I could tell he probably did not know the Lord personally. So, I inquired further.

Gradually he changed the subject to his product, and we discussed the product for twenty minutes or so. He was about to conclude our conversation when I asked, "Could we go back to our original conversation? Tell me more about your spiritual journey and where you feel you are?"

He told me of his background in which he was raised in a particular Christian tradition. I shared how Christ came not to give us a religion but to have a personal relationship with us.

I asked him if he had ever made a personal commitment to Jesus Christ by confessing Christ as his Savior and asking Him to live in his heart. He said he had never done this. "What do you think keeps you from making such a commitment?" I asked.

"Well, quite frankly, I am a controller. I feel that I can't let go of control. I fear what might happen," was his reply.

I let him know that I appreciated his honesty. We discussed at length that every person has a control issue to deal with. Control is a human condition that desires to negatively impact our lives. However, Christ requires us to give up control in order to give us real life. It is the great paradox of faith in Christ.

"So, now that we have dealt with that issue, is there any reason you would not be prepared to make that commitment to Christ?" I gently pressed him.

"Well, now that you put it that way, no, I guess there isn't." Bill prayed with me the sinner's prayer right then, over the phone. What he intended to be a typical sales call became a call that changed his eternal destiny.

That if you confess with your mouth, "Jesus is Lord," and believe in your heart that God raised him from the dead, you will be saved.

Romans 10:9

Work Was Redeemed
by the Blood of Christ

*For God was pleased to have all his fullness dwell in him,
and through him to reconcile to himself all things,
whether things on earth or things in heaven, by making
peace through his blood, shed on the cross.*
(Col. 1:19-20, author's emphasis)

*And Jesus said to him, "Today salvation has come to this
house, because he also is a son of Abraham; "for the Son of
Man has come to seek and to save that which was lost."*
(Luke 19:9-10 NKJV, author's emphasis)

*In Him we have redemption through His blood, the forgive-
ness of sins, according to the riches of His grace which He
made to abound toward us in all wisdom and prudence,
having made known to us the mystery of His will, according
to His good pleasure which He purposed in Himself, that in
the dispensation of the fullness of the times He might gather
together in one all things in Christ, both which are in
heaven and which are on earth—in Him.*
(Eph. 1:7-10 NKJV, author's emphasis)

WORK TO MINISTER

There is also the evangelistic nature of work. It can become a
platform for ministry. In this case we actually work to minister.
Work can also be a means for giving money to the church and
other Christian causes in order to influence societal transformation. A Gallup Poll revealed that 50 percent of people surveyed
in the workplace had discussed spiritual issues over a twenty-four
hour period. The workplace is a natural place to discuss a number

of issues, not the least of which is a person's spiritual condition. Paul is one example:

So he reasoned in the synagogue with the Jews and the God-fearing Greeks, as well as in the marketplace day by day with those who happened to be there (Acts 17:17 NIV).

The apostle Paul was both a workplace minister and a vocational minister. Paul teamed up with Priscilla and Aquila (see Acts 18). They came from Italy and were tentmakers like Paul. Priscilla and Aquila colabored with Paul on many of his journeys. We know they were mature believers because they invited Apollos to their home and "explained the way of God to him more adequately" (Acts 18:26 NIV). God is calling for this kind of partnership with pastors, church leaders, and workplace believers today. Together we can serve the needs of the Kingdom of God through our unique gifts and in our spheres of influence.

My own experience has confirmed the powerful way God desires to use workplace ministry today.

I think we can all agree the role of the pastor is to shepherd the sheep. Ephesians is very clear:

MAKING THE MAIN THING THE MAIN THING

It was he who gave some to be apostles, some to be prophets, some to be evangelists, and some to be pastors and teachers, to prepare God's people for works of service, so that the body of Christ may be built up until we all reach unity in the faith and in the knowledge of the Son of God and become mature, attaining to the whole measure of the fullness of Christ (Eph. 4:11-13).

The problem we are facing in the body of Christ is that the

BE AWARE OF UNUSUAL CIRCUMSTANCES

*Now to each one
the manifestation
of the Spirit is given
for the common good.
To one there is given
through the Spirit the
message of wisdom,
to another the message
of knowledge by
means of the
same Spirit.*

1 Corinthians 12:7-9

We should have a heightened sense of awareness that God is doing something when something unusual happens in daily life. I shared at our ministry board meeting, that God is raising the spiritual bar for Christians who want to impact the world for Christ today. He wants to break through into people's lives, giving them supernatural insights into others' needs in order to bring them to Christ.

A few days later one of our board members, Doug, needed to take a flight. He barely made it on time and was hurriedly taking his assigned seat in economy when he was informed he was being upgraded to first class. He wondered why because he never flew this airline. However, he gladly accepted.

He found his seat, occupied by a lady who wanted to exchange seats. Agreeing, he moved a row back next to an executive who seemed to be a very successful and wealthy person, though very irritated. Doug pondered what God might do as it seemed unusual but divinely orchestrated.

"Lord, tell me something about this man so that he will know that it is You," he quietly prayed. Just then the words financial services popped into his mind. Now Doug had to decide whether this was God answering his prayer or just his own thoughts? Stepping out in faith, he decided to risk it and turning to the man Doug said, "I understand you are in financial services."

The irritated executive looked at him and said, "Yes I am—how in the world would you know that?"

Doug was amazed himself at God's work, and after asking if the man really wanted to know, he replied, "The Lord told me."

"What?" the executive questioned.

"Well, I prayed, and asked God to tell me something about you. God told me specifically your line of work."

The man was not sure what to make of this, but engaged in a conversation with Doug. It turned out the man was the CEO of one of the largest financial services companies in the U.S. During the flight Doug shared about the integration of faith with work and business. The man did not accept Christ, but he experienced a touch of the Kingdom of God It was a supernatural seed-planting encounter.

average Christian has relegated ministry back to the vocational minister. They have never fully taken the mantle of ministry for themselves personally. We cannot place the blame of this condition of the church solely on the pastors.

Most pastors I know want to see their people engaged in personal ministry where they are called. The problem lies in a barrier between equipping that really engages the workplace believer, disobedience of the believer, and affirming and commissioning the workplace believer. Research reveals that 47 percent of believers feel that Sunday morning preaching is irrelevant to their daily lives.[1] This means that our preaching must be made more relevant to the world we live in every day. This will require more effort among church leaders to understand their target audience's world.

This is standard operating procedure in advertising in order to convey the right message about products being promoted. That is why focus groups are used to determine response to advertising messages. Pastors must then develop preaching in order to equip the people in how to apply the Word of God in daily life experiences.

How Do You Define Ministry?

One of the mistakes many pastors make is in how they publicly define ministry. It is normal to talk about the "ministries of the church." We have a women's ministry, a children's ministry, an elderly ministry, and so forth. However, if we are not careful we communicate to church members that anything that is not a formalized ministry inside the four walls of the church is not ministry. This is dangerous. It sends a subtle message to people that what they do from 9 to 5 is not valid ministry and is of lesser importance.

> We have attempted to transform our cities for years without success because we have not equipped those who have the authority to transform our cities. When we recognize and affirm the apostles in the marketplace we will begin to see the transformation of cities.
>
> —Dr. Peter Wagner

Church leaders must reinforce *as a ministry they are called to*, the role of workplace believers in their places of work. Some pastors feel that if they do this they will lose their volunteer base. This has not been found to be true. In fact, it has been the opposite. When believers feel validated that their work life is valued by church leaders, they are more motivated to be involved in other areas.

The Nuclear Church and the Extended Church

I will never forget my first meeting in 2000 with Dr. Peter Wagner, theologian and expert on church growth and trends in the church. My pastor set up a meeting with him to discuss the faith at work movement. "So, tell me about the faith at work movement," said Peter.

"Well, it is quite simple. What we are talking about is that each Christian's work is a ministry unto itself. We do not need to work *to* minister or give more money to the church's ministry activities, our work *is* ministry because each of us is providing a service to mankind through our work. The word *ministry* actually comes from the Greek word that means 'service.'"

Peter took issue with me and argued that since people were not sharing the gospel every time they worked, then it could not be considered ministry. Eighteen months later Peter had totally reversed his position after giving more study to the subject. He is now one of the greatest advocates for the faith at work movement. He has made some insightful observations:

> *For years we have sought after transformation of our cities. We have prayed, held pastor prayer conferences, prayer-walked our cities, etc. Still, not one U.S. city has been*

Workplace ministry will be one of the core future innovations in church ministry. He reported that … a growing number of people will team with work associates to develop a ministry to the people whom they encounter in the workplace …

—George Barna[2]

50

transformed. Why is this? I feel I finally know the answer to that question. It lies in the fact that pastors and church leaders do not hold the authority in the cities where the change must originate. Business and government leaders hold that authority. So, until we in the church equip and release the apostles in the workplace, we will never see our cities transformed by Jesus Christ.[3]

Peter also makes some insightful distinctions between two forms of church life. The *nuclear church*, where many people attend Sunday mornings, has a rule book or culture that is unique. The church in the workplace, or the *extended church*, also has a unique rule book or culture. Those who are part of the church in the workplace understand both rule books. However, church leaders in the nuclear church often do not understand the rulebook in the extended church or the needs and the opportunities that the workplace—as a mission field for Christ—presents the workplace believer.

Now I plead with you, brethren, by the name of our Lord Jesus Christ, that you all speak the same thing, and that there be no divisions among you, but that you be perfectly joined together in the same mind and in the same judgment (1 Cor. 1:10-11 NKJV).

REDEFINING THE TARGET AUDIENCE AND THE LANGUAGE USED TO COMMUNICATE TO THEM

One of the major changes the workplace movement is undergoing is to be more inclusive regarding our audience—from the executive to the majority audience—the nurse, the construction worker, the stay-at-home mom, and the student. For years the nature of our vocabulary and the style of our communication have narrowed the appeal of the workplace message to a limited audience—the businessperson, or those in business. While that audience does need our message of hope, the workplace movement goes beyond that important, but limiting group, to the majority of the workplace constituency—inclusive of all workers.

Defining Our Target Audience— the Top 2 percent or the Masses?

Doug Spada of His Church at Work, cites that, "Many times the language used in the movement excludes workers in government, not-for-profits, education, sports, entertainment—even professions like medicine, where practitioners loathe to identify themselves as 'business people.' This is not a call to 'business ministry,' it is a call to encourage every believer that the work of their hands and minds is their service to God! Ask the person in the workplace whether they consider themselves to be a 'business person' or 'in business.' Try it! You will quickly realize the dilemma. Plumbers, nurses, teachers, construction workers, laborers, and so forth, do not connect with these terms. Neither do professors, engineers, scientists, or members of the armed forces—and what about the millions in local, state, and federal governments?

"We have found that using terms like *workplace* or *work life* instead of marketplace provides an inclusive representation of all who work. True, there are times when *marketplace* is descriptive of the business and executive audience and is appropriate. However, we believe that using the term *workplace* is a term anyone can identify with."

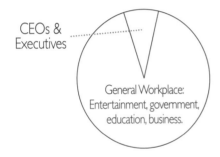

CEOs & Executives

General Workplace: Entertainment, government, education, business.

Full-Time Christian Work

I have often heard vocational workers share a testimony that goes something like this: "I worked in a secular job, before the Lord called me into full-time ministry." Whenever I hear this I cringe. I want to immediately ask, "Oh, were you only a part-time Christian before this time?" This may seem like a small thing, but a lot of small things add up to a big thing. And workplace believers already feel like second-class citizens spiritually. A few other phrases that fall into this category are "I'm in the ministry" and "I'm in full-time Christian work." A better phrase would be "I'm in vocational ministry."

Phrases like these further contribute to the hierarchal view of work and ministry. Whenever someone uses one of these I want to ask: "So I guess I'm not in full-time Christian work if I am not paid ministry staff in a non-profit organization?" Enough said on this issue. I just wanted to encourage you to be aware of language that can communicate the wrong message to those in the workplace.

THE ROLE OF PARA-CHURCH WORKPLACE MINISTRIES

God is birthing workplace ministries around the globe daily. Twelve years ago we could only identify about twenty-five formal non-profit workplace ministries. These consisted mostly of membership groups targeted to Christian businessmen. Today, our *International Faith and Work Directory* (see www.icwm.net, Directory) lists twelve hundred various types of workplace-focused ministries. This is incredible growth and is further evidence that God is up to something. It is also evidence that the movement has largely moved outside the walls of the local church.

Many years ago when mostly men began to see that their

faith life could be lived out in the workplace, they began to get excited about this. Many went to their local pastors and shared their enthusiasm. The local pastor was excited that this person wanted to bring his faith into his work life. However, the pastor did not know how to really help him. The local church did not have any "programs" that fit this model of ministry. So, the workplace leader found himself in a dilemma. The result was that these enthusiastic believers found a deaf ear and decided to do something about it. They realized if they did not do something, their passion would die. So, many began ministries outside the walls of the local church.

When this happened, many local church pastors saw this as competition. They saw it as a threat to their own congregations and rather than encouraging and equipping these people they stiff-armed them. This created a wall between the workplace believer and the church leader. It further encouraged the independent, entrepreneurial spirit of the workplace believer who was accustomed to pioneering new things.

Today I believe there is a paradigm shift emerging. Pastors are beginning to sense there is a genuine move of God taking place. However, they are not sure how to put their hands around it. They just know that something is up. These early-innovator pastors are the Issachars (they recognize the signs of the times) in the body of Christ and are responding. They are encouraging the movement and wanting to learn how to involve their local church.

One leader of a para-church ministry said, "All ships rise when the tide rises." What he is saying is that this movement is going to happen whether church leaders want it to or not. It is coming and we all need to get prepared to embrace it. Those who respond now will be the churches that attract workplace believers. If we don't respond positively, the workplace leaders will go elsewhere. They will seek out the local church that has the kind of focus that can meet the felt need in this important area of his or her life.

THE IMPORTANCE OF WORKPLACE MINISTRY AMONG YOUTH

Young people need to understand this message so that we do not duplicate the sins of our fathers. Many in my generation are having to reverse the sins of prior generations regarding faith and work issues. However, I fear we often send the wrong message to our youth that the greatest calling they can have is in "full-time vocational ministry" instead of helping them see the value of being a godly attorney, singer, journalist, or doctor.

If we are going to see the transformation of our workplaces and culture, we must have strong, committed believers in those places of influence. If we as parents do not model our work as ministry, we will be propagating the sins of earlier generations and the cycle will not be broken. We must teach our young people a biblical work ethic and understanding of work that is not biased toward a hierarchy of spiritual calling.

IS MEN'S MINISTRY ANOTHER NAME FOR WORKPLACE MINISTRY?

Men's ministry is not another name for workplace ministry. In fact, I am struck by how little focus men's ministry gives to work-related areas. For the last four years I have been involved at the leadership level of the national men's ministry movement. Each time I participate I am struck by the fact that men's ministry is not addressing what I feel is the primary felt need among men, which can open the door to every other area of their lives. That need is to help men bridge their faith life to their work life.

Doug Sherman understood the need when he said: "If Christ is not Lord of my work, He will never be Lord of my family."

If that statement is true, then we must decide what changes this requires of our church or para-church ministry.

I shared Doug's statement in a recent workshop at a men's ministry conference. At the end of the workshop a man came up to me and said, "When you shared that statement I began to think if it was true in my life. I realized for the first time that is exactly what happened in my life. It was not until I began to integrate my faith into my work life that it began to penetrate every other area of my life."

It really is not rocket science when you consider the following questions:

▲ Where do the *majority* of men spend the *majority* of their time interacting with the *majority* of the world?[5]
Answer: *The workplace.*

▲ Where do most men gain most of their self-esteem needs?
Answer: *The workplace.*

▲ Where does the authority in the city lie that has the potential to transform cities and society?
Answer: *With those in the workplace.*

▲ Where is the central nervous system that must be captured to change a man's heart?
Answer: *Giving a man meaning and purpose in his work.*

▲ What types of problems are discussed more than 50 percent of the time in small groups among men?
Answer: *Work-related issues.*

▲ In what one area of their lives do men have a 50 to 80 percent dissatisfaction rate?
Answer: *Their work life.*

Indeed, as with first-century Christianity, it all begins in the marketplace, where the disciples of Jesus daily rub shoulders with the lost.

–BILL MCCARTNEY
PROMISE KEEPERS[4]

▲ What causes more stress on a man than any other area which often gets brought home to his family?
Answer: *His work life.*

▲ Men are wired to conquer. What is the one area that they are required to conquer more than any other?
Answer: *Their work life.*

▲ What issues do most men's ministry deal with today?
- Fathering
- Marriage
- Pornography
- Integrity
- Discipleship/Evangelism

I am convinced men's ministry will affect these areas only if it helps men learn to integrate their faith life with their work life first. It is one of the major *keys* to opening a man's heart. Could it be we are not reaching men because we are not appealing to them at their greatest felt need?

How Can Men's Ministry Impact More Men and Really Transform Their Workplaces, Families, and Nations?

We will impact the men in our churches by equipping them to live successfully in the place where they spend 60 to 70 percent of their waking hours. We must appeal to men on the basis of making their faith life and work life integrated and purposeful by bringing Christ into the most important area of their lives.

Here are a few tactics for you to consider for the integration of workplace issues into men's lives.

- ▲ Invite speakers for men's retreats, monthly breakfasts, and one-day workshops that can minister to men's needs related to their work life.

- ▲ Ask men in your congregation who are effectively integrating their faith life with their work life to share a personal testimony in church or at men's meetings.

- ▲ Partner with workplace ministries to resource your men as a part of their core ministry to men.

- ▲ Begin to focus teaching and preaching on faith-and-work related topics within your local church.

- ▲ Let your men's ministry become the champion of the workplace ministry focus in your church for everyone, not just men.

There is a heart cry among men and women in the body of Christ. This heart cry relates to a desire to want to experience God and be used of God.

LETTER TO A PASTOR

Many of the revivals and awakenings that have taken place started in the marketplace. One revival began in 1858 in New York and spread across the country because of the faithfulness of one person in the marketplace. Near Wall Street, Jeremiah Lanphier started holding a noonday prayer meeting in 1857.

That was the beginning of the movement that resulted in the greatest spiritual awakening in America—more than one million people were saved. (For a more detailed account of this event and other biographies of workplace people, please see Appendix 2.) This man's church equipped him and commissioned him. Many believe the same thing is beginning today. Henry Blackaby wrote: "In the Bible, most of the activity of God that changed society was done in the workplace and not in the church." [1]

Since the majority of people spend 60 to 70 percent of their waking hours in the workplace, it is vital that we discern how God wants to use all this time and workplace opportunity. I believe many people desire to understand biblical principles about their work, and how they can relate to the spiritually hungry people in their workplace so that they can ultimately introduce these people to Jesus, and then equip them in their church.

These people need to be taught to become effective ministers at work—to grasp the reality personally—that our relationship with God is not separate from our "work." Those in the workplace hunger for the help, affirmation, and endorsement of the local church. Could the following letter have been written by one of your church members?

Dear Pastor,

For some time now I have felt the need to write you this letter. Let me first say I want to thank you for what you do in helping me learn more about how I can grow in my relationship with Jesus. Your contribution to my spiritual life is so important and is greatly appreciated.

But, there are times I think that you and I may have a wrong view of each other. For instance, as a person in the workplace I sometimes feel I may be valued for the financial contributions I can make, or the ministry position I can fill "at church." Pastor, this makes me feel disconnected and devalued. I know God has created me for a unique purpose, and like you, He has called me for a special ministry.

I know God has given me spiritual gifts and I believe that we should all contribute to the local church function, as well as to the broader Kingdom. Sometimes I feel that the church spends more time equipping me to do the church's ministry instead of my ministry. I love our church and I really have a heart to serve. Can you help me reconcile these feelings? I want to understand and fulfill my purpose—my life ministry.

God has begun to show me something very important. My work is my ministry. I feel that God has called me to be a minister at the workplace, in the same way He has called you to be a pastor. I really see my ministry at work as an extension of your ministry and our church. We don't often discuss ministry in this fashion, and sometimes I sense that my ministry at the workplace does not seem to fit the mission and philosophy of "ministry" in our church.

You see, I believe my ministry is to my coworkers who have never been inside a church building. They don't really relate to "church," so my primary hope of reaching them is by ministering to them at and through work. I may be the only "Jesus" they ever see. Pastor, I wish you could see the people here at work—they are so open to talking about spiritual things.

As I read the Bible, it seems like Jesus spent most of His time reaching people in the marketplace. You have taught me to follow His example and I am finally beginning to understand what you have taught from Ephesians 4:11-12: "And He Himself gave some to be apostles, some prophets, some evangelists, and some pastors and teachers, for the equipping of the saints for the work of ministry."

I agree with you, that as my pastor, God has assigned you the responsibility to equip me for "the work of ministry." God has revealed to me that my greatest ministry is at work. I need your help and training so that I can fulfill my "election" and calling. I know I need more biblical teaching about how to respond to this assignment to a vast, relatively untapped mission field.

Wouldn't it be great if I and other members of our church saw ourselves as "on a mission" at work? Christians taking a position of spiritual authority in the workplace! Just think of the impact the members of our church could make. This would be true multiplication! Pastor, I know you have a desire to see our congregation reach more people for Christ. If we were committed to reaching the largest mission field in the world—our workplaces—just think what could be done.

Wow! It's exciting to imagine what God could do through an army of excited, motivated Christians accountable to the local church as workplace ministers. We might really begin to fulfill the great commission in a revolutionary way. Please Pastor, train us and send us out! Please consider commissioning those of us that are ready as fellow ministers in the workplace.

I love you and appreciate all that you do. I hope that together we can reach the people in my workplace.

> *Very truly yours,*
> *church member*

IMPLEMENTATION OF WORKPLACE MINISTRY IN THE LOCAL CHURCH

*I*n 1998 I received a phone call from a man who asked if he could meet with me. He had found me on the Internet when he was researching the workplace movement. I asked a few probing questions. He was surprised at the level of detail in my questions and the insight I had about his problem. The reason I knew more about his situation is I had walked the same path only a few years earlier. Our relationship immediately began at a deeper level because of the common adversities we had shared in our family and work life. ▶

In the midst of the difficulties God was doing something in his heart. God had given him a heart to learn more about God's activity in the workplace and its relevance to the local church. God gave him a special love for pastors and he wanted to serve them. During the next few years God would birth a new ministry through Doug Spada called His Church at Work. It is designed to come alongside the local church leader to help them understand how they can better equip their people in the local church to release them into their ministry through their vocation. In this next section we are going to deal with how the work life calling should be integrated into the fabric of the local church. I believe Doug is on the front line of understanding what churches should do and not do in this regard.

LAUNCHING A WORK–LIFE MINISTRY IN YOUR LOCAL CHURCH

Today, many Christians live schizophrenic lives, balancing commitments to church, home, and work, often relegating God to the former. But, as Dallas Willard has written, "There is truly is no division between sacred and secular except what we have created. And that is why the division of the legitimate roles and functions of human life into the sacred and secular does incalculable damage to our individual lives and the cause of Christ." Indeed, there should be no distinction between our devotional life and our daily life.

This is reasonably elemental theology, and almost every church would embrace it, but when it comes to *preparing* people for Monday morning ministry—for executing the tenet to live out our faith daily—there is a gaping hole in most churches. That hole, more positively-conceptualized as a discipleship opportunity, involves preparing people to live their faith at work, or what we call "work-life ministry."

Few churches offer anything resembling an on-going ministry in this area. Often, the closest they come is an effort focused on the white-collar business community—a "marketplace ministry," a businessmen's small group, or a 7 A.M. executive prayer breakfast. In doing so, they minister to the 5 percent who are leaders in

by Doug Spada and Dr. David Scott,
His Church at Work.org

their work environments and ignore the 95 percent who are not.

That's tragic, we think, not only because this 95 percent are left with little guidance about what it means to be a Christian at work, but also because this majority is surrounded every day by untold legions of non-Christians and nominal Christians to whom they could reveal God. Seemingly, the church is missing one of its greatest opportunities for both discipleship and evangelism. At best a church attracts a few hundred, perhaps a few thousand people each week. Its members, on the other hand, have contact with twenty times that many people in their typical workday.

Work-life ministry fills this gap, assisting believers to see God's agenda for their work lives and teaching them to steward their time, talents, and relationships in God-honoring ways. What does that look like in operation? And what tools exist to help a church create such a ministry? From our experience with launching these ministries in local churches around the country, here are several essential steps.

A ROAD MAP FOR LAUNCHING A WORK–LIFE MINISTRY IN YOUR CHURCH

Lay a Foundation of Prayer. Any effort is in vain without the blessing of God's Spirit. Start the ministry with a campaign of prayer and undergird its ongoing efforts with continued intercession.

Appoint an Active, Passionate Leader. A work-life ministry needs a "champion," a delegated, activist leader, whether a lay member or a person on staff. This is an absolute prerequisite for success here. Next to God's blessing and the pastor's support, identifying the right individual whom God has raised up is fundamental to the whole effort.

If you are interested in launching such a ministry, but you're not in your church's leadership, begin persuading the decision-makers that this ministry should be a priority. Share with them your vision and passion. Pass on to them the books, tapes, and articles that have opened your eyes to the paradigm of work-life ministry. Begin praying for them. Invite them to go with you to a work-life related conference. Connect them with other churches who are successfully implementing work-life ministry strategies. God may very well use you to help them catch a whole new vision, and you may be the key to the reformation of your church.

Add "Work-Life Equipping" to Your Church's Objectives.
A work-life focus ought to be a central theme integrated into the mission of your church. A one-time programmatic emphasis will probably falter. Work-life equipping is not an event-driven campaign, but a long-term initiative that, if done properly, yields abundant fruit.

Build a Strategic Framework.
Carefully consider what it is that you want to do and what it will take to do it. What's entailed in equipping your members? And how will you deliver that information? How will you go beyond imparting information and encouragement to generate real passion for living out the faith at work? Without a structural framework in the church sustainable action is difficult.

One place to start is *www.HisChurchatWork.org*. Besides offering conceptual models, His Church at Work also provides a set of turnkey practical tools and strategies that many churches are finding helpful. The organization helps churches develop the framework for an ongoing process of work-life ministry coming alongside church leaders and their delegated work-life champion to help create and launch the ministry. That includes, among

At best a church attracts a few hundred, perhaps a few thousand people each week. Its members, on the other hand, have contact with twenty times that many people in their typical workday.

DOUG SPADA AND DR. DAVID SCOTT

67

other things, creating a vision, a team, the graphics, a unique set of online tools, a plan for long-term success, and the on-going support of your ministry.

Promote the Work-Life Ministry. Without visibility, a work-life ministry will not engage and mobilize people in the church. It needs a name, a logo, and a communication infrastructure. It requires promotion in church communications like bulletins, announcements, the church Web site, newsletters and emails.

We suggest a month-long, church-wide emphasis to get the ministry onto the average member's radar screen. The ultimate goal is to integrate it into the entire culture of the church. Sermons cast the vision from up front and lay the groundwork of the basic biblical precepts. Involvement tools and online resources help people get on board.

Avoid Vocabulary That Can Derail Your Message. Ultimately, work-life ministry is a paradigm-shifting effort. For everyone to get the message that their "work matters to God," we must choose our rhetoric carefully. The question is not what you think you are saying, but what your audience actually hears. Much of a Christian's confusion about their jobs can be traced to the stumbling block of our vocabulary.

For example, be careful how you speak of "ministry," taking care to not unwittingly exclude the spiritual significance of "work." Even well-meaning categories such as "spiritual gifts," "evangelism," "tithing" and "missions," when given singular emphasis, can leave the impression that work-life only matters as a means to the end of "real ministry."

Use inclusive language that communicates to the entire work-force spectrum of your church. Most would not describe themselves as "business people," "executives," or even "professionals." Also in describing the ministry, talk about "work-life" rather than "workplace" ministry because not every worker has a workplace, *per se*. But every worker does have a work-life.

So audit the cumulative message and language of your church. Ask yourself, what are we really communicating to our intended audience?

Keep Work-Life from Becoming Just a "Niche" Ministry.
By nature it is catalytic. All Christians need equipping for a Christian work life. Youth must be prepared for it. Singles, couples, men and women all struggle with it. Senior citizens face significant adjustments related to it. Accordingly, this ministry should cut across and resource almost every other sector of traditional church programming and ministry: adults, youth, families, evangelism, prayer, small groups, and preaching. The transformational potential of a work-life ministry outlook will probably not be realized if it's relegated to a special interest group ghetto.

Launching and sustaining a work-life ministry in the local church requires a shift in a church's strategic thinking. It requires envisioning a whole new ministry landscape for the local church. Tall order, for sure, but the payoff is far greater. Consider this: the true scope of influence for any church is not its attendance, but the sum total of the relationship networks of its members, most of whom work. If each person has regular interaction with twenty other people during a given week, then a church of 250 has a potential scope of influence of 5,000, and a church of 5,000 has a potential reach of 100,000! Work-life ministry grows out of the vision to steward this wider ministry opportunity. Its task is to

THE PAYOFF

mentally and practically merge the ministry of the church with the daily ministry of its people.

Such a ministry has other payoffs as well. It will not only accelerate the growth of your church, it will enhance the spiritual maturity of your church members. Moreover, members' appreciation for their church will likely deepen as the church relevantly speaks to the daily challenges people face and as it equips people for their calling. It keeps God in front of them, empowering them everyday. In one church where they launched a work-life ministry, a member wrote to the staff a message that is typical of the outcome here: "Our workplace ministry and the tools are a great encouragement for me throughout the week. This is an awesome ministry and it helps me to stay focused on what's really important. Thanks to all that are involved!"

Surely, the church that makes a priority of work-life ministry will have no problem filling its pews. Beyond that, though, it will be filling its pews with more authentic disciples—people equipped to take that 9 o'clock Sunday message and apply it at 9 o'clock on Monday morning.[1]

ESTABLISHING ENCOURAGING RELATIONSHIPS

Chapter Eight

Therefore, since through God's mercy we have this ministry,
we do not lose heart. —2 Corinthians 4:1

by Kent Humphreys

Pastor Greg Walters sat at his desk, staring at the opposite wall; it had been a long day. The daughter of one church family had just lost a five-year battle with leukemia, and her funeral had taken place this morning. Although the day itself was sunshiny glorious —the cemetery decorated with autumn's crown of red and gold— and the church had turned out en masse to comfort and support the girl's parents, these things were always hard. Greg felt drained, knowing that he, too, would miss the giggly ten-year-old.

Greg had taken some time after lunch to think, read his Bible, and pray. Extra time with the Lord always renewed his peace, strength, and positive attitude. This afternoon he had counseled a couple preparing for their marriage (a happy hour), followed by a counseling session with a young man battling anorexia (a sober and troubling one). Starting to feel weary, Greg looked forward to the Wednesday evening church dinner, Bible study, and prayer time.

After that, he would be presenting several new ideas to the Personnel Committee. It was now 10 P.M., and Greg should be home. Instead he sat in his office, feeling a mixture of agitation and concern. Robert Miller had not been at the Personnel Committee meeting, calling Greg at the last minute to apologize

71

that he had to work late. Could he catch up with Pastor Walters over lunch in a few days to discuss the new issues? Of course, Greg had said yes, but he was more frustrated than he had let on.

Robert had no way of knowing how excited Greg had been to present his new ideas and how ineffective the meeting had been without Robert present, but the problem went beyond that. Greg worried about Robert's focus on work. Could it be that his focus to make money was growing stronger than his focus to love God and his church? Robert's desire to be included and to participate in the church's programs *seemed* to be as strong as ever, and his wife and kids still came to everything, but more and more often Robert seemed preoccupied with work, and he had recently missed several events such as tonight's meeting. Maybe Robert's promotion to CEO had gone to his head.

Greg had thought about this dilemma before—so much so that he had asked Cheryl, another of the church staff members, if she had sensed anything wrong with Debbie, Robert's wife. She had not noticed anything different about Debbie's demeanor but would make it a point to listen more carefully at the weekly women's Bible study. Cheryl did mention that during a recent conversation about how hard it was to get the kids to church when Robert was out of town. Debbie had seemed to take it in stride, expressing gratitude, in fact, that Robert was situated where "God wanted him."

Cheryl had gone on to say that she *had* noticed a similar pattern with Susan Voight, who had bought a boutique a year ago. Susan had been so excited about it but was now having trouble keeping up with all of her obligations in the church's women's ministry. To make matters worse, Tracy Barrington had recently gone to work for Susan, and Cheryl was concerned that she, too, would experience the pull of two worlds.

Greg wondered whether it would always be this way with business-oriented people. Could they not be leaders at work and in church at the same time? It was a confusing situation, at best, and would take more thought and prayer.

At 10 P.M. that same evening, in an office across town, Robert Miller sat at his desk, staring at the wall opposite him. What a day! He had been elated when his promotion to CEO had materialized, because he had long felt a need to find ways to show Christ"s love to the people he was around every day. Now he had the authority to make things happen for good for his employees as well as their families. He felt tremendous responsibility for them and had been praying that God would give him direction.

Robert wanted the company atmosphere to be that of an extended family, and he was trying to be sensitive to people's needs. He hadn't expected what happened next. As folks became convinced that he really did care about them, they began to let him see some of their personal battles. Just before closing time today, Jim, the man whose office was next to Robert's, poked his head in the door.

"Can I talk to you for a minute?"

"Sure, come on in."

After excusing himself for a minute to call the church and let the pastor know that he wouldn't be there for a Personnel Committee meeting, the two men settled down to talk. Robert worried about missing the meeting because he knew that new business would be presented, but he would call Pastor Walters tomorrow to explain.

Guilt gnawed at the edges of his thoughts. Jim's benign comments initiated two hours of revelation of heart-wrenching fear

I was called up front to the church to commission me as the teacher for the school age children for the year. Later I wondered why I have never been recognized for teaching kids five days a week as a ministry.

SCHOOL TEACHER

and worry; Jim suspected that his son might be an alcoholic and that his daughter was probably sexually active with a boy whom he loathed and distrusted. This man had been trying to run the operations of a multimillion-dollar firm today while his mind was waging war for his kids. Robert listened, talked a little, and prayed with Jim, who seemed to be more settled when he left.

It was obvious to Robert that he needed to find more help for Jim, someone he could talk to regularly and who knew more than Robert did in these areas. Where would he find such help? He needed to find help for Mark and his family, too. Mark, who lived in another state, was a salesperson for the company. He had an important territory, and the work could not be entrusted to better hands.

Mark was a hardworking man of integrity and honor. But this morning he had found out that his cancer, which he had thought was detected early and could be easily treated, had actually metastasized throughout his body. Mark had very little time. His family was devastated. Robert had to act fast to help this family and to help the company. If a family ever needed to know Jesus, it was Mark's family—now.

Robert realized that this was a huge opportunity to share God's love with them, and he would. He would also look into the health insurance issue tomorrow. How could they take care of Mark's widow? What kind of care did Mark need now? Who could he send to handle Mark's territory?

Then there was the matter that had been brought to him by the warehouse manager. The company had recently hired a number of people, many of whom did not speak English. They were good workers, and fortunately enough of them could communicate with the manager and each other to provide efficiency.

Yesterday, one of them had asked the manager if he knew of a minister who could perform a wedding; they were new to the area and did not have a church. They also hoped the minister could visit a family member in the hospital. It seems the mother had difficulty with a home birth, and both she and her baby had to be rushed to the hospital and admitted. The extended family was frantic due to a lack of understanding about what had happened and how the hospital system worked.

Robert knew that something must be done for them, possibly for the whole community. He could visit the family with an interpreter, but the help must go beyond that. Maybe having a chaplain who came regularly to the company would be a start. He would look into that and other solutions, too. He needed time to think and pray.

Robert was overwhelmed with excitement that his prayer to be able to influence people around him for God was being answered, but he was also anxious about what to do next with all of these opportunities. He wished he had someone to talk to about it. The logical person would be Pastor Walters, but Robert had ambivalent feelings right now about the church. He suspected his only use there was to provide money and a presence in committee meetings. He felt no one understood the dilemmas he faced, and he fought guilt over lacking time to be more involved. It seemed right that the church should be the place to turn to for ideas regarding ministering for the Lord, but Robert could think of no programs or classes there that would remotely address those issues.

These hypothetical scenarios are repeated over and over in real churches and businesses. It is a tragedy that people such as these, who have so much in common, rarely cross paths except to greet each other in a hallway at church or to briefly chat about surface interests. What would it look like if they were to join their considerable forces to minister to the workplace while strengthening the effect of the church in the community?

THE DILEMMA

Let's begin by looking at the common issues that both you, as a pastor, and the workplace leader face. Both leaders are in upper management of their respective organizations, and both can feel "alone at the top," isolated. They feel the pressure of being responsible for many people who look to them for vision and wisdom. They both need encouragement but find few, if any, people with whom they can communicate honestly. They both work hard with great intentions but often find their motivations misunderstood.

So the question that continues to pull at my heart is this: if we (pastors and workplace leaders) have so much in common, why haven't we tried to understand each other and work together? Although many reasons contribute to the common gap in relationships between pastors and business leaders, a few stood out in the results of our surveys.

First, there is the phenomenon I call the *intimidation factor*. Many people who are influential in their businesses feel intimidated by the spiritual life of their pastor. It is a puzzle: in the business world they can hold their own, but when comparing themselves to their pastor on the platform every Sunday morning, they think they could never match up. Conversely, pastors can be intimidated by workplace leaders, especially the high-powered executive types. There is a fear of the control that they can exert by use of their personalities or their money.

Second is the *vulnerability factor*. The simple fact is that deeper relationships require a certain level of openness. Most people fear vulnerability, and men have a harder time with it than do women. One pastor put it this way: "I find it difficult to talk about my own insecurities and feelings of inadequacy, and I have achieved this level of vulnerability with maybe four men in the church at different times. It is risky."

That pastor is correct; it is risky. After all, if I reveal my open and honest self to another, what will the other do with the information? Will I be rejected or misunderstood? Will the information inappropriately be shared with another? We must come to realize that such relationships are worth the risk. Even Jesus sought the intimacy and encouragement of sharing His most important moments with a trusted few. Although Jesus had a huge congregation, only Peter, James, and John were invited to share the Mount of Transfiguration experience or the prayer time in the Garden of Gethsemane.

Jesus had the most critical mission and carried the greatest burden of responsibility in history. He experienced time pressure and was inundated with crises to solve, yet He made a point to develop a few trusted relationships with whom to share not just His ministry but also His life. We need the same. It is a fact that the lay leaders in your church could be your greatest encouragers, and you could be the spiritual support system that they need as they learn to minister in their workplaces. I believe that God has something to say to us.

Many people who are influential in their businesses feel intimidated by the spiritual life of their pastor. It is a puzzle. In the business world they can hold their own, but when comparing themselves to their pastor on the platform every Sunday morning, they think they could never match up.

THE SOLUTION

What would happen if you were to choose a few workplace leaders from within your own church and meet with them regularly? The goal of such a small-group meeting would be to help these leaders figure out how to have an effective ministry in their own spheres of influence, while mentoring and encouraging them spiritually along the way.

These meetings would involve both praying and looking in the Bible for answers, but most of the ideas for marketplace ministry would come from the brainstorming of the leaders themselves. The leaders will be the greatest resource you have, although there are various other resources available to help accomplish your goals.

First, you, as the pastor, pray about which leaders—starting with just a few—to invite into your initial group. Then, meet with each one individually *on their turf*. For example, meet one at the office for a brief tour and then take him or her out to lunch. Present your invitation and ask that leader to pray about joining you and a few other leaders for this experimental group. Set the date for the initial meeting approximately three weeks in advance so that the participants can clear their calendars and you can make these lunch dates without haste.

Meet during lunch or breakfast time, weekly or biweekly, somewhere out in the marketplace. It usually works well to have lunch at the office of one leader, having sandwiches or pizza brought in to conserve time. The meetings start out with folks sharing ministry ideas and basic biblical principles; then, as time progresses, these people become vitally important to each other. They merge into a support group like none of them has ever had before. The leaders learn how to support and encourage you as their pastor, just as you are learning how to help them. The results are exciting.

In *TGIF Today God Is First*, a series of marketplace meditations, Os Hillman quotes a Third World pastor: "We've spent too much time equipping our workplace people to do our ministries rather than equipping them to do the ministry God has called them to in the first place … . The workplace is the greatest mission field of our day, and yet we do not train our workplace leaders on how to effectively integrate faith into their workplace … . God is removing the wall of separation by speaking to pastors and workplace believers all over the world."[1]

Like Jesus in the first century, this Third World pastor understands that the greatest ministry opportunity today may be through workplace leaders. Recently, I received an e-mail from Ron Elliott, a Midwestern pastor, who told the following story:

> *I visited with one of my laymen [Doug] last night— He has a heart for the Lord and is very gifted in evangelism. He is a taxicab driver and probably works seventy hours a week. He shared with me how he has the opportunity to share with many people each day about Christ. He has more opportunities to share Christ in a week than I have in a year.*
>
> *He has a Bible study with about ten to fifteen cab drivers on Thursday evenings in the basement of the Omaha public library. (The owner of the cab company is not a Christian and didn't want them to have the Bible study in the company building.) Doug's manager is a Christian and participates in the study. Doug is beginning to develop a vision of reaching cab drivers for Christ.*

This is an interesting and innovative ministry I never would have thought about. I had Doug share in church last night what God is doing in his life. Over a year ago he asked the church to pray for a cab driver who was addicted to gambling. That cab driver approached Doug two weeks ago and said, "I am ready." Doug said, "Ready for what?" He said, "I am ready for God."

Doug had the opportunity to lead him to the Lord. This is what excites me as a pastor—seeing my flock going out during the week where they live and work and impacting their sphere of influence for Christ. This is what it is all about. Doug has a strong and clear vision of what his ministry should be. Because he has a plan and is time-efficient, he also has time to heavily support Pastor Elliott and his church. It is a win-win situation for both men. Not only do they have a mutual need for each other, but they are also enjoying the mutual benefits of having a close relationship.

Q&A Isn't this whole idea becoming more intriguing to you? I would like to finish this chapter with several questions that various pastors have asked.

Q: *Why do I need to be the one to initiate this?*

A: Jesus' example to us was such. When He wanted to impart His ministry to people, He could have gone to church leaders. We know from history that at least a few such leaders were open to Him, Nicodemus being one of them. But Jesus chose leaders from the market place. Some were already acknowledged public leaders, such as Matthew, and some were leaders only in their own small realm, such as Peter. Jesus went to each of them on their own turf and invited them to join Him. Then He spoke to them in terms that they understood while they learned to understand spiritual terms. (With Peter, for example, He used fishing terms.) He trained them in their world until they were ready to train others and carry on the mission.

Q: *What advantage would there be for the church if I do this?*

A: First, the church's ministry expands when workplace leaders are set loose to impact their world for Christ. It gives a boost to the ultimate fulfillment of God's Great Commission to us.

Next, the church gains leaders who are more productive and less crisis-driven. They have a plan, and so their decisions are no longer driven by the tyranny of the urgent because they now have a way in place to deal with it.

Finally, the flourishing of outreach ideas will impact others not involved directly with the small group, and the church's outreach will grow.

Q: *What advantage is there to me?*

A: As a pastor, you gain loyal and supportive friends who truly do understand you. A few of them will become your closest confidants. You need them as much as they need you! You also gain focused volunteers for your church programs and for the community in general, not fragmented souls who have good intentions but cannot pull life together into an organized whole.

Q: *Would workplace leaders really go for this idea?*

A: Yes, they would and they have. The fact is that many business-people have tried to accomplish this for themselves, meeting weekly in the marketplace to brainstorm and encourage each other, because they have not been offered such help by their churches or their pastors.

Q: *What sacrifices would I have to make in order to accomplish this? After all, life is already too busy.*

A: There is a time sacrifice. Something else may have to be limited or omitted from your schedule in order to do it. Initially, there is thinking, praying, and planning time. Then there is an hour for each individual you invite. After that, there is an hour every week or so (depending on how you plan it) for regular meetings. Otherwise, the time demand is flexible, depending on your desired involvement with the individuals or their ministries. There is always an emotional cost of being involved with people, but in this case, the primary emotion is excitement rather than discouragement.

Q: *Exactly how could time be carved out for such a task?*

A: The best times for meetings of this nature are lunch hours and early mornings because people frequently have those times free. It does not add an extra hour during already busy evenings and weekends.

Q: *Can you train men and women together?*

A: Yes, you can. There are distinct advantages to having both sexes involved in your groups. Women have an easier time being open with their feelings and ideas. Their intuition is a God-given ability that men typically don't possess, so they add important input. On the other hand, men often can see the big picture and the possible pitfalls of ideas more easily than women can. We need each other.

You must consider, of course, that when you work with a combined group, you decrease the opportunity for intimacy in sharing and it usually takes more time to achieve trust with confidentiality. Because of these factors, men-only and women-only groups are the most popular in the present workplace environment, but try to keep your mind open to various possibilities that God may want you to try.

In conclusion, I'd like to share with you my life verse, Philemon 1:7: "For I have come to have much joy and comfort in your love, because the hearts of the saints have been refreshed through you, brother" (NASB). Wherever God has placed me, I have sought to encourage those around me. As we fellowship around the person of Jesus Christ and His Holy Word, may we be encouraged together.

As workplace leaders and pastors, we all have a tendency to be loners and to not open ourselves to intimate relationships with others, particularly those in our own organizations. May God allow us to find each other and to renew and deepen relationships, thus building a foundation for true spiritual fellowship and equipping.

Action Steps

1 Target individuals in your church who are leaders in the marketplace or in your community. They may or may not hold positions of leadership in your church. Spend time with God, asking Him to give you these names.

2 Quietly and informally start relationships with these individuals apart from any church program. Plan to spend a morning a week having breakfast with one or two of them together. Spend this time simply getting to know them better. Set a luncheon date and go by their offices and tour their workplaces. They will expect you to have an agenda such as fund-raising or the start of a new program. Your actions will mystify them.

3 Drop them a personal note or card encouraging them about what God is doing in their lives, stating that you are praying for them or thanking them for their friendship. You might put this book down for a couple of weeks while you think about all of this. You may want to give a copy of the book to a pastor friend with whom you would like to do this project. Take your time. What you are doing is important—establishing encouraging relationships.[2]

CHURCH CASE STUDIES

When we think about implementing work life ministry into a local church environment, we must realize there are varied ways this can be accomplished. There are a few major components for any church that is going to be successful in this. First, it must be intentional and it must become part of the DNA of the local church. In other words, you must make it part of *everything* you do because this is not just another program to be selected as an *a 'lacarte* offering by your members. It must be part of the philosophical fabric of the local church body—from *how you speak* to *how you equip* to *how you affirm and commission* your people.

The following case studies reveal how unique each approach can be for different kinds of churches.

FOUR CHURCHES THAT HAVE SEEN FRUIT BY IMPLEMENTING A PHILOSOPHY OF WORK LIFE MINISTRY

Wooddale Church

Eden Prairie, Minnesota

Wooddale Church is a suburban church located in the Minneapolis, Minnesota area, which launched a whole body work-life ministry in February of 2003. The average weekly attendance is five thousand. The church is intentionally influencing approximately thirty thousand unchurched people in the workplace through the work lives of their congregation each week.

Ginger Johnson, the work life director at Wooddale, explained what has taken place since they began an intentional focus on workplace ministry:

Through owning a unique small part-time business I had numerous opportunities to connect one-on-one with clients as well as with colleagues from thirty-seven countries. God allowed me to experience almost daily ministry encounters through my work-life connections. I needed support and help as I walked and lived as a workplace minister! In addition to my work life I also was very active within the ministries of my local church.

About four years ago I approached my church with the conviction that there were many other people in our church pews who needed support and encouragement in the workplace! We agreed to launch a group in our church for this purpose called "Evangelism Entrepreneurs." About six of us met weekly and prayed for an entire year while this initiative took shape. We had pastoral support, publicity, and three to four gatherings during that year. About twenty individuals would come out each time— usually the attendance being different people each time. Keep in mind we had a congregation of about five thousand. We had a great time sharing, teaching one another, and dreaming about how to more effectively spread this to others in our congregation.

However, after about a year of this it seemed that the effort it took and the lack of being able to *sustain* the group and ideas, and so forth, just made it too unmanageable and too much work to continue. The church and I had a sense that there was some better way that we had not put our finger on. Was our niche ministry all there was? It helped such a limited few. We abandoned our efforts.

About a year later God connected us to a bigger picture. We learned about a "whole body" work-life process and infrastructure that was available to support the dreams of our church in this area of the workplace.

Since launching our Work Life Ministry at Wooddale Church

> Wooddale Church launched its workplace ministry, and the impact has been significant! I have had many calls, e-mails and people stop me in the hall to tell me their appreciation of various aspects of the ministry. At this point, nearly 20 percent of our five thousand weekly church family are engaged with our workplace ministry and now are taking steps to grow and impact others at work.
>
> GEOFF BOHLEEN
> OUTREACH PASTOR
> WOODDALE CHURCH
> EDEN PRAIRIE, MN

in partnership with the planning, services and turnkey tools of His Church at Work — our church now has over twelve hundred people engaged in work-life ministry at one level or another. We have the vision, tools and system to affirm and equip our people for life transformation in the extended church—on mission within the workplaces all across our city!

Yes, we still have some big events and niche type workplace elements. We still have ministry to the unemployed. We still have small groups and more. Just *a lot* more of them! And many of them occurring *in* the workplace itself and not on the church campus! So, it is critical to see beyond a niche workplace ministry or tactic that helps a relative few to a transforming "whole body" work-life ministry that affirms and helps the whole church.[1] *www.WooddaleatWork.org.*

Journey Community Church

SAN DIEGO, CALIFORNIA

In 2001, Journey Community Church launched one of the first intentional church-wide workplace ministries in the nation under the leadership of Doug Spada, the director of that church ministry. With a weekly attendance of approximately twenty one hundred, Journey Community Church is intentionally influencing approximately sixteen thousand unchurched people in San Diego workplaces through the work lives of its members. The church process God birthed at Journey became the inspiration and foundation for many church-wide ministries now being launched nationwide through the vision of HisChurchatWork.org.

Journey is an influential church with the ambition of reaching the city of San Diego for God. It has implemented a strategy for reaching an expansive area of San Diego County, attendance is growing, and it is known in the community as a healthy, healing church. Rick Warren's Purpose Driven Church division awarded Journey its "church health award" several years ago.

Journey continues to look for creative and biblical ways to reach the community with maximum effectiveness. In following with the principles of *A Purpose Driven Church*, Journey viewed a church-wide strategy of work-life ministry as a natural and dynamic way to reach a large portion of the county. The church views the impact on members' lives as a critical indicator in the effectiveness of this focus.

As the work life ministry at Journey continues to mature the church looks for more ways to drive the truths of "work as a true ministry calling" deeper into the DNA of the church. To elevate this issue, the church devoted an entire month in 2003 to equipping each member for his or her calling at work. A month-long series called "The God of Monday—Finding God in Your Workplace" was developed and then taught by Pastor Ed Noble. Drama, discipleship, and testimony were all part of this pervasive work-life campaign.

The work-life ministry continues to grow and become a vital part of Journey's Purpose Driven strategy.[2]
www.JourneyatWork.org

Sonset Baptist Church

GRAPEVINE, TEXAS

Ron O'Guinn is the pastor of Sonset Baptist Church in a community near Dallas, Texas. Ron founded Allofus Ministries, a ministry that is focused on reconciliation among races. He is a former

> Our workplace ministry and the tools are a great encouragement for me throughout the week. This is an awesome ministry and it helps me to stay focused on what's really important.
>
> JOURNEY MEMBER

director of reconciliation for Promise Keepers. Ron is also a former businessman who worked at Motown Records during the heyday of soul music. He worked with people such as Diana Ross.

Ron attended the April 2003 "His Presence in the Workplace" conference held at the Billy Graham Training Center and came away from that conference with his eyes opened to a whole new way of looking at things. "It was like the veil was removed from my eyes," said Ron. "I can't believe I have not seen this before. It makes all the sense in the world. I have failed to equip my people to really see their work as a ministry." Ron was so impacted by the conference he immediately went back to his small congregation in his bedrock community and began to implement immediate changes.

First, he made a change in his own life regarding workplace ministry and his own workplace—his church. He decided that every person with whom his church came into contact—including the postman, the UPS man, repairmen, and so forth—needed to experience the love of Christ personally through that contact. Second, he began to equip and affirm those in his congregation that their work was a ministry and a calling. Third, he decided to begin pastoring the city. That meant he did not wait for people to come into his local church building; instead he began to reach out to the community in very creative ways. He began a program he calls the "Business Marketplace Enhancement Program."
The purpose of this initiative is twofold.

▲ To analyze every workplace represented in his church and to visit these workplaces and their employees and begin to pastor them just like he pastors every church member.

▲ To make available a twenty-two step ministry to them that

involves everything from transportation for employees who can't get to work to childcare to wedding and funeral services for the unchurched.

Ron explained that he saw every member in his congregation as a potential church plant. This change in philosophy has revolutionized his ministry. He recently had a major corporation president call him and ask him to come pray over the new business year. The CEO was not even a member of his church. But because he saw something unique in Ron that was bringing faith into the workplace, the CEO was drawn to him. "We are no longer ministering to the church, we are now ministering to the community. This is an entirely different approach for us and it has become part of the DNA of our church," said Ron.

One of Ron's "membership clients" is a local restaurant. Ron visits the restaurant regularly and pastors the employees. The owner of the restaurant is appreciative of this special touch from Ron—so much so that he gives Ron a special table in the restaurant to bring his guests. There is also a side benefit to Ron—he gets to eat free! He loves that part of the deal!

Ron has taken this a step further. He wrote a proposal to the governor and the mayor of his city asking that the Sunday before Labor Day each year be recognized as Business, Commerce, and Labor Appreciation Day. He wants to recognize the contribution of working people and the enhanced value they bring to the community. Ron is only one pastor of a small community church who is making a difference in his community by taking a proactive approach to viewing the workplace as a mission field. He is actively planting churches in the 9 to 5 Window of his community.

Brunswick Church

TROY, NEW YORK

Not every church takes a formalized approach to workplace ministry. Some pastors simply make it a part of their DNA in the way they minister to their flock. Following is an interview with Pastor Harry Heintz of Brunswick Church in Troy, New York. He has been pastoring this church for twenty-nine years.

Question: You are considered a church that emphasizes that its people are all ministers and have been sighted as a model church in the faith and work movement. What makes you different from other churches in your ministry model?

Pastor: We believe in the priesthood of all believers. In a practical sense we live this out in many ways:

▲ We are less programmatic and more comprehensive in our approach. A program often isolates those who are not interested in the program and you contribute to the segmentation problem again. A programmatic method often tends not to spread to the entire congregation if it does not have the interest of the entire body. We teach and repeat the philosophy in all we do and say.

▲ We've abolished the term "laity" because we don't believe it is biblical unless used of everyone.

▲ We don't use titles such as reverend, doctor, or the minister, but we believe in the office of pastor and are fine with using pastor.

▲ We don't elevate our vocational pastors spiritually above others who are also called in a bi-vocational way.

> Even the most committed Christian is only attending church an average of two times a month according to a Gallup poll. It's a lot like preaching to a parade.
>
> DR. EDDIE GIBBS
> FULLER SEMINARY PROFESSOR

91

▲ Everyone is on a first-name basis.

▲ We always enforce the idea we are all ministers.

▲ Our corporate prayer focus is "community" prayer, not just from pastors, though often led by pastors.

▲ We are careful with our language so as not to isolate believers who are not paid by the church.

▲ We commission our people on a regular basis to the work place on a par with overseas missionaries.

▲ We open the pulpit to others inside our congregation who demonstrate a gift for preaching. We are always training people inside our body in their gifts.

▲ Every worship service concludes with a clear charge to daily ministry.

I believe the whole movement is about the Reformation's emphasis on the priesthood of all believers. We have a team approach to sermon development. I work on sermons a couple of months in advance. I have meetings with a team of staff and non-staff people to discuss and pray about issues that should be preached. These all have mixed vocations in order to give the preacher perspective on the topic. This team meets weekly to do serious biblical spadework. The one who will be preaching takes notes and listens.

About once a month I pick one person in the congregation to spend the day with at their workplace to learn what they do and I observe. This gives me a great education on what the people in my congregation face every day.

When asked why more pastors don't embrace this concept,

Pastor Heintz suggested two reasons:

> **Institutionalism:** *The body has become more institutional-ized than organic. We are often more concerned about survival than pouring ourselves out for others.*

> **Hierarchal:** *We have become caught up in this stuff. I believe control on the part of the pastor is at the center of this. I have learned a lot from reading books about Southwest Airlines and Jim Collins's books,* Built to Last *and* Good to Great. *The CEOs in those companies actually have it together better than many of the pastors in our churches today because they manage in a less hierarchal manner.*
>
> *I believe most of the congregation I serve understand their calling. Our pastors are treated like regular people rather than elevated to a higher spiritual plane. We are constantly developing other preachers in our congregation that can speak in the pulpit. Currently about half of our preachers are professionally trained (seminary) and about half, actually a little over half, are amateurs, doing it for love and trained locally.*

A Pastor Who "Left the Ministry"?

Ike Reighard is an unusual example of a pastor who understands the faith at work movement and has become a central figure in helping pastors understand how they can integrate this message into the fabric. In 2003 Ike made an incredible career change when he stepped down from the senior pastor role of NorthStar Church which he founded in Kennesaw, Georgia, a suburb of

Atlanta. Ike began serving the community through his local church and came in contact with HomeBanc mortgage company. He began pastoring the CEO and the staff; he spoke at retreats and community functions.

Ike's ministry became "market-focused." When HomeBanc began interviewing for the position of Chief People Officer, the CEO, Pat Flood asked for his assistance in interviewing for the position. When Ike read the job description he said: "You have just described me!" That led Ike to make a big career change and take the position of Chief People Officer at HomeBanc. He still preaches once a month at NorthStar as the founding pastor. His peers thought Ike had lost it. His growing church had grown to more than twenty-five hundred members and was taking off. Reighard commented on this movement:

> *Every day in America the vast of majority people get out of bed and travel to one of two locations. As a student they go to school, or as an adult they go to work. I believe these two daily destinations are where the greatest opportunity lies for ministry in today's culture. Over 60 percent of an adult's waking hours are spent going to work, being at work or traveling home from work. The cutting edge church of today and tomorrow knows this and capitalizes on these facts.*
>
> *As the Chief People Officer for HomeBanc Mortgage Corporation and Founding Pastor of NorthStar Church I have my feet firmly planted in both arenas. I am watching God do an amazing work in the spirituality that I am seeing in the workplace. I am having the time of my life seeing God work in the lives of people everyday.*

When a local church equips and commissions their workplace believers to see their work as a calling and a ministry, their church becomes alive. People get excited about the fact that they no longer have to feel guilty about being in a secular job and that their vocations are more than a job.

When the church leaders reinforce this, it wins the workplace believers to that local body. They become more willing to plug into that local body because they are being appreciated and affirmed for their workplace calling. Every person likes to be affirmed. When we affirm people's place in ministry, they begin to walk in their callings and contribute to the Kingdom of God in ways they never realized they could. The local church becomes what it has always been designed to do—equip believers for the work of ministry.

TEN WAYS TO SUPPORT MINISTRY IN THE WORKPLACE

by Pete Hammond

Where is the church on Tuesday? Do our church members view themselves as agents of the Kingdom of God where they work? How can a congregation better affirm and mobilize its pew-sitters in ministry within their jobs?

Pete Hammond directs Ministry in Daily Life for InterVarsity Christian Fellowship. He is one of the early pioneers of the workplace movement and has developed the following ten ways church leaders can help equip and mobilize workplace believers in their callings.

1 *Dedicate or commission members from various industries on a given Sunday.*

One option is to design worship on Labor Day around the responsibilities and positions your members have Monday through Friday. Members or selected representatives could either wear their work clothes or bring items from their jobs for a dedication ceremony. Also, a slide show could be presented portraying various members at work.

2 *In the public pastoral prayer include intercession and/or thanksgiving for key industries.*

Pray for particular difficulties such as a downturn in business, a strike, disaster, or a major challenge they might be facing. Have members serving within that arena stand during the prayer. The prayers of thanksgiving could rotate through various sets of people and affirm their calling and service to the larger community (teachers, managers, public servants, transportation workers, retailers, social workers, workers in the area of finance, food-service workers, and so forth).

3 *Clergy should have patterns of visitation to the workplace just as they do with the sick, bereaved, or homebound.*
Some call this "shadowing." You spend a few hours with a member at their workplace as a silent guest. You would not be introduced as a pastor, but as a friend. Afterward, the two of you could have coffee or a meal and explore what you observed. This will enlighten and enrich your work in the Scriptures, counseling, and preaching—while affirming your people.

4 *Create a pattern in the educational ministries of your church where classes, study groups, seminars, or evening institutes are shaped around workplace issues or affinity groups.*
Some could be formed around specific industry groups (educators, managers, government work, health care, law and justice, manufacturing, retailing, and so forth) while others could be formed around workplace responsibilities (supervision, finance, administration, sales, ethics, philanthropy, management, leadership, and so on).

5 *Small groups could be developed throughout the congregation around workplace affinities in industries or responsibilities.*
These could meet for breakfast, happy hour, weekends or even within the Sunday school time for prayer, accountability, encouragement, study, case studies, and problem solving. Pastors could attend as advisors and learners.

6 *The church could sponsor employment helps such as a career guidance event, a job hunting and availability bulletin board, a care group for the unemployed or transitioning members, or internships for young people at members' places of work.*

7 *Establish congregational communications that feature news about members in their work.*

Options include a bulletin board, a column in the church newsletter or bulletin, a prayer chain or hotline, and so forth. Items could come from the local newspaper, business publications, photos taken by friends, awards received, job promotions and changes, or workplace news stories with a note listing members who are in that industry. Other items could be occasional profiles of biblical personalities that were in various industries. In the church member listing add the industry (not the organization because these change frequently) of each working person.

8 *Sponsor special "learning experiences."*

These might be a children's day at work with their parents, workplace storytelling, testimonials or panels in children's Sunday school classes, or seminars, mini-retreats or workshops on various themes about work. A "bring your boss or coworkers to worship" Sunday could be sponsored.

9 *Equip the church library bookshop or resource center with helps on work and faith connections.*

There are many good books (over two hundred currently), videos, publications, and curricula now being published. Do a regular feature or review of these in the church publication to inform folks of topics and availability.

"One of the greatest hindrances to the Christian's internal peace is the common habit of dividing our lives into two areas—the sacred and the secular. But this state of affairs is wholly unnecessary. We have gotten ourselves on the horns of a dilemma, but the dilemma is not real. It is a creature of misunderstanding. The sacred-secular antithesis has no foundation in the New Testament."

A.W. TOZER
THE PURSUIT OF GOD

10 *Do a sermon series on workplace themes from the Bible.*
It could feature profiles of various people (Lydia in the clothing trade; Daniel, Deborah, or Joseph in government; Nehemiah and Ezra in construction; Priscilla and Aquila in affordable housing; Job and Jacob in agribusiness; Matthew in finance, and so forth). Another approach could use various themes and issues such as money, power, ethics, witness, management, service, conflict, and so on. You might establish a review group of working laity to work on these sermons with you. You could also build in a brief lay response of application, testimony, or critique to your sermon. *(See Appendix 2.)*

We need to help the church function seven days a week. Our members are the delivery system for the Kingdom's salt and light. The recognition and support of the workplace ministry of our people is a challenging and rewarding venture that deserves all the affirmation, understanding, and guidance we can muster.[1]

REACHING THE 9 TO 5 WINDOW:
Twenty-six Action Steps You Can Take Right Now

The following ideas and strategies can help you begin to mobilize men and women to see their work as a calling and ministry from God.

1 Establish a team of intercessors to pray for workplace believers, businesses, and pray for God to establish a ministry to workplace believers in your church.

2 Present real-life examples of workplace transformation—to inspire personal application in different types of workplace environments. (*See Appendix 2.*)

3 Preach sermons related to workplace applications. (Form a team of workplace believers from different vocations to give input on the type of sermons that should be preached to address the needs of those in the workplace.)

4 Conduct a survey among those in the church that asks this question: How might our church help you apply your biblical faith in the context of your daily work life? Provide five specific things the church could do.

5 Start an ongoing workplace ministry/outreach that mobilizes your entire congregation into the workplace. "His Church at Work" can launch a *Work Life Support Center* online for your church. *www.hischurchatwork.org*

TWENTY-SIX ACTION STEPS FOR THE LOCAL CHURCH

6 Preach a series of messages on the priesthood of all believers in the context of work. Preach on the five-fold ministry in Ephesians 4 and how these gifts and offices are found in the workplace.

7 Remove formal titles of church staff that would tend to place them spiritually above members in the church. Reinforce the concept that each person's call is equal in the sight of God. (This does not mean church leaders are not the spiritual leaders and shepherds.)

8 Avoid addressing or favoring only those "in business" or those with influence. Equip and train the whole workforce for ministry in the workplace. Including mothers, students, executives, construction workers, and professionals.

9 Affirm workplace believers that their call is equal to a vocational ministry call in its spiritual importance.

10 Understand the problem that often separates workplace believers from church leaders. This will help you see the heart of a workplace believer.

11 Affirm workplace believers through church commissioning services focused on the church recognizing and confirming their calling (vocation) in a formal way.

12 There are hundreds of workplace ministries that can be a resource for your local church. See our *International Faith & Work Directory* listings on page 195 and our complete listing online to identify workplace ministries that can assist you in your geographical area. These ministries can often provide helpful advice and equipping resources.

13 Provide discipleship opportunities for your people. Several workplace ministries offer online devotionals. My *TGIF Today God Is First* is a free daily e-mail devotional that helps men and women apply biblical faith in their daily workplaces. It also represents a great source for sermon ideas: *www.marketplaceleaders.org* Marketplace-Network is another resource: *www.marketplace-network.org*

14 Ed Silvoso offers an "Anointed for Business" conference that also provides excellent teaching on what it means to transform the workplace for Christ. I also teach a one-day workshop, "Called to the Workplace," that is designed to equip your workplace believers to see their work as a ministry. *www.marketplaceleaders.org*

15 Begin a small-group ministry in the workplace. Priority Associates, Priority Insights, and Needles Eye Ministries are three ministries that have excellent resources and tips on how to host a successful small group in the workplace.

16 Read books on the movement and make them available through your church bookstore. See each workplace ministry's selection of products and books. For a complete selection of resources visit *www.faithandworkresources.com.*

17 Establish a SWAT team of intercessors from your church willing to go into businesses and pray for the leaders. Their role is to go into different businesses to help discern issues that may be hindering God's blessing upon the business.

18 Place a workplace emphasis on your missions or outreach budget in order to focus your church in this area. You can also support workplace ministries of your choice that equip men and women in the workplace such as the International

Coalition of Workplace Ministries (ICWM) which services the entire movement.

19 Marketplace Network specializes in equipping the professionals and career-minded in your church. A "How To Start A Marketplace Ministry in Your Church" kit is available to help you get started with Bible studies and other resources designed for this audience. *www.marketplace-network.org*

20 Begin to encourage your people to see their work as a ministry through preaching, teaching, and equipping. (See Appendix 2.)

21 Study successful church models that are operating based on these philosophies. (See Chapter 9 and see *His Church at Work & ICWM* site for models of church-based ministries.)

22 Invite guest speakers to speak on faith and work issues to introduce your congregation to the movement and their unique calling to their vocations.

23 Download PowerPoint presentations by Os Hillman and Rich Marshall that can be used in teaching and training. *www.marketplaceleaders.org, www.icwm.net* and *http://www.godisworking.com*

24 Once a week spend a few hours with one member in his place of work for a few hours. Get a feel for the struggles and opportunities in his workplace.

25 Teach a theology of work to your young people so they do not have to relearn God's view of work.

26 Allow one or two people each week to stand up and share a brief testimony on how they experienced God's presence in their workplace that week.

I teach students who spend $40,000 to learn a language that no one understands.

Dr. Eddie Gibbs
Fuller Seminary professor

WHAT IS THE END GOAL? TRANSFORMATION

Chapter Twelve

TEN PARADIGM SHIFTS TOWARD COMMUNITY TRANSFORMATION

by Eric Swanson

A small cloud is on the horizon. The winds of change are beginning to gather strength and with certainty a storm is coming—change is coming. All over our world there is a quiet movement of the Spirit of God that is causing believers to re-examine how they "do church." Churches are throwing out the old measures of success. It's no longer merely about size, seeker sensitivity, spiritual gifts, church health, nor the number of small groups. It's about making a significant and sustainable difference in the lives of people around us—in our communities and in our cities.

There is a growing awareness that we cannot continue to do the same old things and expect a different result. If we want to be the salt and light, we as the Church were created to be, we have to do something different—we have to be something different! Community transformation is not found in programs, strategies, campaigns or tactics. For most of us it will take nothing less than a shift of seismic proportions in what the Church is to be in the 3rd millennium.

A paradigm is a model consisting of shared assumptions regarding what works or what is true. A paradigm shift is that "aha!" moment when one sees things in such a new light that one can never go back to the old ways again. Each paradigm shift takes us from a model of thinking that we must discard to a new model that we must embrace. A new paradigm is the new wine-skins that will be needed to hold the new assumptions about what is true. To maximize our impact on our communities—urban, suburban or rural, we need changes in at least ten of our paradigms of how we currently view church.

1 *From building walls to building bridges.*
"You are the salt of the earth—You are the light of the world" (Matt. 5:13,14).

The first paradigm shift pertains to where we, as the church, see ourselves in relation to our communities. Will we remain outside of the community inviting people in or will we go to our communities, seeking to be a transforming agent? The church is called to be separate in lifestyle but never called to be isolated from the people it seeks to influence.

For many years founding pastor, Robert Lewis, of Fellowship Bible Church (FBC) in Little Rock was content to be growing a successful suburban mega church. By his admission, FBC was a "success church." Success churches seek to grow by having attractive programs and offerings that people can come to and benefit from. But Robert grew increasingly dissatisfied with the impact FBC was having on the community. So he made an appointment with the mayor of Little Rock and asked one question, "How can we help you?" The mayor responded with a list of challenges facing the greater Little Rock area.

FBC then challenged themselves with the question, "What can we do that would cause people to marvel and say, 'God is at work in a wonderful way for no one could do these things unless God were with them?'" That one question was the first step in becoming what Lewis calls a "bridge-building church." For the past four years, FBC has joined with over one hundred other churches and over five thousand volunteers in the greater Little Rock area and served their communities by building parks and playgrounds and refurbishing nearly fifty schools.

They set records for Red Cross Blood donations and have enlisted thousands of new organ donors. They began reaching out to the community through "LifeSkill" classes (on finances, marriage, wellness, aging, and so forth) in public forums like banks and hotel rooms, with over five thousand people attending.

In the past four years the churches of greater Little Rock have donated nearly a million dollars to community human service organizations that are effective in meeting the needs of at-risk youth. They have renovated homes and provided school uniforms, school supplies, winter coats, and Christmas toys for hundreds of children. After getting new shelving for her classrooms, one school principal said, "I think this is the most fabulous day of my life as far as education is concerned. I've been in this twenty-nine years and this is the first time a community or church project has come through for us."

The churches of Little Rock have let their light shine in such a way that Jesus Christ is made real to the community. Once a church makes this mental shift regarding how it lives in its community, it is only limited by its creativity in how it can serve its community and be the salt and light it was meant to be. It makes the transition from providing ministry programs for the community to forever changing its relationship to a community.

I've been working for seventeen years and it's only in the last year or so that I've recognized my workplace as a ministry. How many Christians die without ever realizing the ministry God had for them?

MARK GREENE[1]

2 *From measuring attendance to measuring impact.*
"The kingdom of heaven is like yeast ... mixed into a large
amount of flour until it worked all through the dough"
(Matt. 13:33).

In a post-modern world most people are neither impressed with
the size of a church or its commitment to "truth." Yet from the
cover of *TIME* magazine to the front page of the *Wall Street
Journal*, transformational community-centered ministries are
grabbing the attention of the American people. Perhaps, in this
century, the greatest apologetic for the reality of Jesus Christ
living in a community will be observational more than proposi-
tional. To have a faith that can be observed is to be living out the
truths we want others to grasp and the life of the Savior we want
them to know.

When Jesus chose one passage to describe His mission and
ministry, He picked up the scroll of Isaiah and read from Isaiah 61:

The Spirit of the Lord is on me, because he has anointed me
to preach good news to the poor. He has sent me to bind up
the broken hearted, to proclaim freedom for the captives
and release from darkness for the prisoners ... to comfort
all who mourn and provide for those who grieve in Zion—
to bestow on them a crown of beauty instead of ashes, the
oil of gladness instead of mourning and a garment of praise
instead of a spirit of despair.

The way He "preached" best was by holistically combining
proclaiming with comforting and providing. This is how Jesus did
ministry. *"The Word became flesh and made his dwelling among
us"* (John 1:14). Likewise, the apostle Paul was as "eager to

108

remember the poor" (Gal. 2:10) as he was "eager to preach the gospel" (Rom. 1:15-17). Effective ministry has always been holistic, combining good deeds with good news (Acts 10:36-38).

When Tillie Burgin started Mission Arlington, her mission was simple—take the church to the people who were not going to church—"to hang out and hover around John 3:16." As she ventured out to meet and minister to her neighbors, she was immediately challenged by Jehovah's Witnesses who told her, "You're invading our territory. Get back into your church building where you belong."

Today Mission Arlington is a house church movement of nearly 250 community house churches (and nearly four thousand in attendance) serving over ten thousand people a week in the Arlington Texas community with food, furniture, medical and dental care, school transportation, child and adult day care, counseling, and so on. What can Jesus do for a community? The people of Arlington know. Every year hundreds of people come to Christ through this transformational ministry. Lives are being touched. Lives are being changed. The church should and can make a huge difference in a community.

Windsor Village United Methodist Church has made a big difference in southwest Houston. From twenty-five members in 1982 Windsor Village is currently the spiritual home for more than fourteen thousand members. Embracing both evangelism and economic development and armed with the belief that every member is a minister, each congregant is encouraged to embrace Jesus' mission of identifying and holistically meeting the needs of those around them.

Under the leadership of pastor Kirbyjon Caldwell the church purchased a 104,000 square-foot former K-Mart that was converted into their "Power Center." Since 1999 the Power Center has had an estimated $28.7 million impact on the community creating over five hundred construction jobs and three hundred regular jobs through the Power Center which serves over nine thousand families a month through Windsor Village's over one hundred ministries. Currently they are engaged in developing a twenty-four-acre planned residential community consisting of over 450 affordable single-family homes called Corinthian Pointe and they continue to make a difference.

In 1988 Vaughn and Narlene McLaughlin moved into a depressed area of Jacksonville to begin a church designed to meet the needs of the whole person. Today their converted Bell South building called the "Multiplex" houses nearly twenty for-profit businesses including the Potter's House Café, a credit union, a beauty salon, a graphic design studio, and a Greyhound Bus terminal, all started by church members who lacked capital but had a dream.

Another building serves as an incubator for two-dozen new businesses. The multiplex also houses a 500-student Christian Academy. In addition to their ministries of economic empowerment and education, they also have nearly twenty-five other ministries such as a prison and jail ministry, youth ministry, Big and Little Brothers, and free car repair. They also have a team of 250 volunteers who "look after things in the city" even if it means to simply sweep the streets of Jacksonville.

Though an outstanding preacher, to Bishop Vaughn McLaughlin, ministry is always what happens outside the church: "If you are not making an impact outside of your four walls, then you are not making an impact at all." In 1999, Bishop McLaughlin was named "Entrepreneur of the Year" by Florida State University.

Is it any mystery why the city and its leaders have so wholeheartedly embraced Potter's House? The question he repeatedly asks is the question that churches in all kinds of neighborhoods are increasingly asking themselves: "Would the community weep if your church were to pull out of the city? Would anybody notice if you left? Would anybody care?"

The question, "How big is your church?" should be replaced with "How big is the impact you are having on your community?" Every other measure is interesting but not relevant. Let's refuse to be impressed by numbers alone. There are many ways to engage the community and make an impact. The only "bad" way to engage the community in service is not to engage at all!

3 *From encouraging the saints to attend the service to equipping the saints for works of service.*
"It is (God) who gave some to be … pastors and teachers, to prepare God's people for works of service" (Eph. 4:11-12).

In the typical church, lay people are asked to serve in five or six capacities:

- Teach a Sunday School class
- Work in the nursery
- Lead a home Bible study or small group
- Sing in the choir
- Be an usher or greeter
- Serve on a board or committee

Little wonder pastors lament that only 20 percent of their members are "active." Could it be that the service opportunities are not broad enough to engage the energies and passions of people in the church? Robert Lewis noted that when people

Christianity is essentially a lay movement founded by a lay Jew who was neither Sadducee (a member of the priestly class, a political aristocrat), nor a Pharisee (a keeper of the law), nor a scribe (an interpreter of the law, a sort of canon lawyer). Jesus Christ was not of the priestly, political, moral or legal elite.

ANNE ROWTHORN
THE LIBERATION OF THE LAITY[2]

entered his church they were excited for about four to five years. How could they not be excited? Fellowship Bible is a teaching church and Robert is an incredible teacher. But he observed that after around five years, people get bored with church if they are not involved in ministering to others. It was not until the church began to serve their community did members find their serving niche and continue in their growth.

Tim Keller of Redeemer Presbyterian Church in New York City writes that the process of mobilizing members into ministers "starts by articulating clearly and regularly a theology of 'every-member ministry' …. From the pulpit, in the classes, by word of mouth, it must be communicated that every layperson is a minister and that ministry is finding needs and meeting them in the goal of the spread of the kingship of Christ."

In the 1980s a small group in Mariner's Church in Costa Mesa, California, met for a year to study every Scripture that had to do with the people of God and the needs of a community. They asked themselves two questions—"What could we do?" and "What should we do?" This was the beginning of Mariner's "Lighthouse Ministries."

Today Lighthouse is employing the volunteer hearts and entrepreneurial skills to minister to the under-resourced people Orange County. In 2001, Lighthouse Ministries employed the dedication and talents of nearly thirty-four hundred church volunteers who gave ninety-five thousand hours of service (the equivalent of forty-six full-time staff!) in the form of tutoring foster children, mentoring motel families, taking kids to camp, visiting the elderly, teaching English at one of their learning centers, working in the Mariner's Thrift Store ($168,000 in sales last year) distributing Christmas gifts, team building with teens at their leadership camp, assistance with immigration papers, working in transitional housing or volunteering with Orange County Social Services.

Despite the prolific use of volunteers, volunteering is simply the avenue to "build relationships with people in our community." Recently they were featured on National Public Radio for their work in providing transitional housing for youth leaving foster care. Last year they touched the lives of nearly twelve thousand people in their community through their relational volunteer ministries. Their mission of "Bringing Christ's hope to those in need" is being fulfilled.

4 *From "serve us" to service—from inward to outward focus.* *"For even the Son of Man did not come to be served, but to serve and to give" (Mark 10:45).*

Several years ago Chuck Colson made the observation that when the Communists took over Russian in 1917, they did not make Christianity illegal. Their constitution, in fact, did guarantee freedom of religion. But what they did make illegal was for the church to do any "good works." No longer could the church fulfill its historic role in feeding the hungry, welcoming the stranger, housing the orphan, educating children or caring for the sick.

What was the result? Seventy years later, the church was totally irrelevant to the communities in which it dwelt. What Lenin did by diabolic design, most churches have done by default. But the result is identical. Church is irrelevant to most people. Take away service and you take away the church's power, influence, and evangelistic effectiveness. The power of the gospel is combining the life-changing message with selfless service.

Marion Patillo is the executive director of a ministry in Dallas

The ministry is for all
who are called to share in
Christ's life, but the pastorate
is for those who possess
the peculiar gift of being able
to help other men and women
to practice any ministry
to which they have
been called.

ELTON TRUEBLOOD[3]

called Metro-link. As the name suggests, Metro-link serves as a "conduit" between volunteers from some forty churches and twenty-seven city blocks in South Dallas. Marion observes that when Metro-link began, there were 955 churches in South Dallas yet the area was rife with crime, alcoholism, drug addiction, and prostitution. Why? It was certainly not from the lack of churches!

The problem centered on the fact that most churches had not been serving this community. It was observations like this that caused Charles Chaney, former head of the Southern Baptist Home Mission Board to remark: "America will not be won to Christ by existing churches, even if they should suddenly become vibrantly and evangelistically alive. Nor will the U.S. be won to Christ by establishing more churches like the vast majority of those we now have." The power of the church is not merely in the number of churches but the focus of those churches.

Mary Francis Boley, was the director of women's ministry at First Baptist Church in Peachtree City, Georgia. Women from metro Atlanta would gather each week around coffee and an open Bible. But the ministry took a radical step forward when Mary Francis decided that no Bible studies could meet unless they included a component of ministry to the community. So they scoured Atlanta for the women in the "highways and hedges" who nobody else was reaching.

They identified cashiers, food service employees, hairdressers, single moms, the women's shelter, strippers, and prostitutes. Mary Francis calls her ministry, "Wellspring of Living Water." The goal of Wellspring is to get the women within the church to reach the women who are outside of the walls of the church. Mary Francis's purpose is to "save the women in Atlanta"—and that begins with the women who are in the pews of the church every Sunday. She firmly believes that people cannot grow into Christian maturity without giving themselves away to others. By ministering to "the least of these" they invite the presence of Jesus into their ministry (Matt. 25:31-46). Lives are being touched and changed.

Churches like Vineyard Community Church of Cincinnati have also found that it is easier and more effective to recruit existing small groups to engage in ministry and service projects than it is to motivate, administer spiritual gift tests, and recruit individuals to serve in a ministry. You can serve in most any ministry with your friends.

Each Saturday Vineyard Community Church sends out teams of people just to serve people in the city through "low touch, high grace random acts of kindness." One day you might find them handing out free Cokes or washing cars for free. Founding pastor Steve Sjogren defines their servant evangelism as "demonstrating the kindness of God by offering to do some act of humble service with no strings attached. It's not so much a matter of sharing information but sharing love."

Senior Pastor Dave Workman notes that their church believes that it takes between twelve to twenty positive "bumps," or refreshing encounters with the church, before people come to Christ. These small acts of service move people toward Christ. Though all service is with no strings attached, each year they see hundreds of people come to faith. Carved in stone over the entrance of the church are engraved the words: *Small things done with great love will change the world*. Steve Sjogren's admonition to church planters is this: "Don't go to start a church … go to serve a city. Serve them with love and if you go after the people nobody wants, you'll end up with the people everybody wants."

First Baptist Church of Leesburg, Florida, (population twenty thousand) has a prevailing influence on their community though their incarnational (John 1:14) ministry which they call "ministry evangelism." The church has spawned over seventy ministries to intersect the physical, emotional, and spiritual needs of the people in Leesburg. Through their Men's Shelter, Women's Care Center, Benevolence Ministry, Latchkey Ministry, the Children's Home, and so on, they regularly lead hundreds of people to Christ and disciple them toward maturity. Senior pastor Charles Roesel (since 1976) said, "The only way the gospel can be biblically shared is to focus on the whole person, with all their hurts and needs, and to involve the church in ministering to those persons and leading them to Christ. This is the essence of ministry evangelism."

Erwin McManus of Mosaic Church in East Los Angeles says that the single biggest factor in his church retaining people is not personal follow-up or joining a small group; it is being involved from the very beginning in service to others in the community. When members have told him that they want the church to meet their needs his reply is: "You are the church and together we are called to meet the needs of the world."

Over eighteen hundred members agree. We grow and are healed as we serve others. Maybe this is what Isaiah had in mind when he penned God's words to His people: *"Is this not the kind of fasting I have chosen: To loose the chains of injustice and untie the cords of the yoke, to set the oppressed free and break every yoke? Is it not to share your food with the hungry and to provide the poor wanderer with shelter? ... Then your light will break forth like the dawn and your healing will quickly appear"*(Isa. 58:6-8).

What if we settled for nothing less than 100 percent of our church members engaged at some level in meaningful ministry to the community? People (or small groups) could choose their field and level of engagement (from once a week to once a year), but noninvolvement would not be an option.

5 *From duplication of human services and ministries to partnering with existing services and ministries.*
"Two are better than one, because they have a good return for their work" (Eccl. 4:9).

Nearly every community has a number of human service agencies that are morally positive and spiritually neutral which are doing their best to meet the needs of the underserved and under-resourced people of the community. Such agencies include the local food bank, homeless shelter, emergency family housing, and safe houses for abused women.

Equally true there are church and para-church ministries that are effective in ministering to specific target audiences (business community, youth, college students, and so forth). Rather than starting a new ministry, why not form partnerships with existing groups as "partner ministries" of a local congregation? Chances are that people from your congregation are already serving in many of these organizations. Why not use the current community energy to create synergy?

The Bible is replete with examples of how God used secular people in partnership with His people to fulfill His purposes. Think of Joseph and Pharaoh, Nehemiah and Artaxerxes, and Esther and King Ahasuerus. Instead of each congregation having its own food pantry, why not partner with the local community food bank? When needy people request food, congregations could refer these folks to their "partner ministry."

In our Boulder County community, Big Brothers Big Sisters

of America (BBBSA) has two hundred boys on a list waiting for an older mentor. Yet how many churches do you know that are saying, "One of these days we'd like to begin a youth mentoring program"?

Why not form a partnership with BBBSA? Let BBBSA shoulder the cost and liability for screening applicants. There is no reason to form a duplicate ministry if the service or ministry already exists and is effective in accomplishing its mission. Imagine how great it would be if your church bulletin included not only the men's and women's Bible study times but also a list of twenty to thirty "Community Partner Ministries" as well.

Maybe we can effectively love our city with the love of Jesus Christ through agencies and mechanisms that already exist! Most human service agencies need what the church could readily supply—caring volunteers, financial support and even facilities. The door is always open for servants wanting to serve and help. We form partnerships not around theology but around our common concern *and love* for the city.

Rick Rusaw is pastor of a twenty-nine-hundred-member LifeBridge Christian Church in Longmont, Colorado. Several years ago LifeBridge made a conscious decision to "care for their community." They invited local human service agencies to office on their campus and encouraged members to get involved in the life of the community. "We're just looking for ways to help the city," Rick explained. "For example we decided we didn't want to start a Christian school but to get involved in serving the needs of the existing public schools of our community. We don't need to duplicate what is already out there."

Last year when a local high school student took his life, the school principal called Rick at LifeBridge and asked if they could

Servants always have access to the palaces of kings.

118

send over twenty counselors for three days to be on campus with the kids. When asked about how they gained such access into a public high school, Rick responds that he sent over the same twenty folks who had been setting up chairs at assemblies and raking the long-jump pit all year long. Servants always have access to the palaces of kings.

Last December over thirteen hundred people from LifeBridge donated thousands of hours of community service over during their "Time to Serve." Partnering with twenty-nine human service agencies and local ministries they cleaned three elementary schools top to bottom and then spent another six weekends fixing up a mobile home park. Five auto mechanics from LifeBridge serviced over three hundred cars of single moms in the Longmont area.

LifeBridge members came up with five thousand ways they could serve their community. Rick sums up his commitment to Longmont: "I used to think I could change the world. Now I just want to change the stream … not by standing on the bank and yelling but by getting in the water. The way to make truth visible is to make 'Christian' a verb not just an adjective." This past year they were on the front page of the local newspaper thirty times (the majority of which were positive!). Their commitment to their community is their letter "known and read by everybody" (2 Cor. 3:2).

6 *From fellowship to functional unity. There is a strong case to suggest that there is really only one Church in a city or community (made up of all believers) that meets in several congregations around the city.*
In Philippians 2:2 Paul implored, *"Make my joy complete by being of the same mind, maintaining the same love, united in spirit, intent on one purpose."*

Only unity of purpose around the vision of a transformed community is strong enough to unite pastors and churches of different denominations.

Jack Dennison of CitiReach wrote:

While solid relationships form the basis for unity, we can't stop there. My observation in city after city is that often-times unity becomes an end in itself. So we see repetitive efforts to demonstrate our unity through citywide worship events, prayer vigils … and other similar events. These activities … are wonderful symbols of our unity but they rarely produce real substance. They make us feel good and sometimes result in great newspaper coverage, but the cities remain unchanged.

Uniting the Church around a common goal is preferable to trying to unite the church around a cooperative project. We align ourselves "in unity to pursue the same goals for our community while each participant determines the part it should play." Functional unity does not exclude cooperative efforts but functional unity also implies that each church can act with a degree of sanctified independence, not waiting for permission from others to serve the community, as long as it is working toward the agreed upon vision of a healthy, transformed community. Community transformation begins at the intersection of the needs and dream of a community, the calling and capacities of the Church and the mandates and desires of God for a community.

In 1990 pastors and Christian leaders in Fresno, California, "fueled by the pain of the city" formed a multisector leadership team and began praying together for their community.

Emphasizing compassion over power this "no name fellowship" was the beginning of unprecedented cooperation not just among the faith community but also between the faith community and other entities serving the city. By "connecting leaders who often never cross paths," what has come to be known simply as "One by One Leadership" is "transforming geography into community" through mentoring, tutoring, job training, community store-house, asset-based community development, welfare to work, police/church partnerships, and a myriad of other civic engagements.

"It works because we love each other, we trust each other, and we hold each other accountable," said Fresno pastor Paul Binyon. Other cities like Houston, Pittsburgh, Jacksonville, Little Rock, New York City, and several others are being changed because the Church is coming together around a common vision for what the city can become through significant ministry and service.

7 *From condemning the city to blessing the city and praying for it.*
Jeremiah 29 begins by saying: *"This is the text of the letter that the prophet Jeremiah sent from Jerusalem … to those I carried into exile from Jerusalem to Babylon."*

What follows are instructions on how to live as aliens in a foreign land. Listen to his admonition: *"Seek the peace and prosperity of the city to which I have carried you into exile. Pray to the Lord for it, because if it prospers, you too will prosper"* (v. 7).

For too long we as the Church have positioned ourselves as adversaries to our communities. The monolithic Church has stood from afar and lobbed in pontific salvos condemning the city and those who are trying to serve it. Maybe it is time we began blessing the city by blessing those who have given

> You see at the moment
> people come to me on a
> Sunday and they're saying,
> "Feed me up, fill me up,
> bandage me up—make me
> ready for another week out
> there." And in a way it's a
> constant drain. But if they
> really saw their work and
> workplace as a context for
> ministry then they'd be
> coming back to the church
> feeding us and filling us with
> all the stories of what God
> has been doing out there …
> The whole church would be
> being refueled, not drained.
>
> REVEREND GARY ROWLANDSON[4]

themselves to the city!

Pastors in our Colorado community have begun inviting city officials and influencers to their monthly lunches. The mayor, the chief of police, district attorney, editor of the newspaper, the university president, and others have spoken to this ministerial alliance. After these guests address the gathering they are prayed over and the ministers thank God for these folks and ask Him to bless these city servants (1 Tim. 2:1-4).

Anyone can curse the city but pastors are in a unique position to really "bless" a city and its people. Each year the Church in Little Rock has honored a different group of servants—the police, firefighters, schoolteachers, and so on at their annual "Share Fest." One year Pastor Adam Hamilton of the United Methodist Church of the Resurrection (COR) passed out the names of every teacher, administrator, and employee of the Kansas City School District—one for each of the fifty-seven hundred people in attendance.

Each person was asked to pray regularly for that person and send a card of encouragement and appreciation. The response was overwhelming! From that one strategic blessing scores and scores of COR members are now volunteering and tutoring the children of Kansas City—and are transforming the city. Perhaps the next great reconciliation movement will be between the Church and the community.

We not only need to bless our communities but we need to pray for them as well. The extent that we will impact our communities will be proportionate to how effectively each influential segment of our community (educators, business, law enforcement, arts, civic leaders, human service agencies, and so on) are being prayed for.

Two-hundred-thirty congregations in Jacksonville are praying daily for every one of the police force through their "Adopt-a-Cop" ministry. Twice a year in Little Rock over a thousand people come together to intercede on behalf of the city. In Houston, Doug Stringer of Turning Point Ministries ("Somebody Cares Houston") said that over 75 percent of Houston's twenty-seven hundred square miles are now covered by daily prayer by the Church in Houston.

It's hard to be adversaries with those you pray God's blessings on. All over our nation, through organized efforts like Concerts of Prayer and Mission America's Lighthouses of Prayer movement, walls are coming down. Individuals and communities are being prayed for. The Church is being reconciled to the community.

8 *From being a minister in a congregation to being a minister in a parish.*
"As Jesus approached Jerusalem and saw the city, he wept over it" (Luke 19:41).

A congregation is made up of people who attend a local church from a community. The minister typically feels that this congregation is his flock whom he must baptize, marry and bury. They consume his time and energy. Being in a parish is different.

A parish differs from a congregation in that it is a geographical scope of concern and responsibility. A congregation is a subset of a parish. So what difference does that make? Being in a parish gives one the God-given right to minister to anyone in the community, whether they are part of one's congregation or not. Urban theologian, Ray Bakke, illuminated this point by writing that every minister has two functions: 1) to be pastor to the members and, 2) chaplain to the community.

Rich is a pastor of a small church in our city. His congregation is seventy but his parish is over ninety thousand! Rich sits comfortably serving between the human service community and the faith community. Rich's office is the local coffee shop. His tools are his cell phone and his laptop. Rich is the person God has used to connect our community leaders to our monthly ministerial alliance meetings. His days are often filled with walking through our city and interceding for it. Isaiah 61:1-6 describes the reward of those who "rebuild ... restore ... (and) renew" the city. It is the city that bestows on them their titles—*"And you will be called priests of the Lord, you will be named ministers of our God"* (Isa. 61:6).

9 *From anecdote and speculation to valid information.*

Two pieces of information changed the course of Nehemiah's life that resulted in the transformation of a community. In Nehemiah 1, he learned that the walls and gates of Jerusalem were broken down and her people were in great distress. These two pieces of accurate information were catalytic to Nehemiah's prayers and plans to restore a broken wall and a broken people. His burden to transform the city came from accurate information.

We too need correct information about the real needs of our community as well as the resources we have to meet these needs. Do we know the demographic information of our community? Do we know the number of churches? Do we know the spiritual history of our community? Ray Bakke said that in assessing community needs we need to identify the people in need (poor, disadvantaged, children, elderly, single parents, disabled, prisoners, sick, aliens, and so on) along with the type of needs they have (physical, spiritual/moral, social, emotional, or cognitive). Most information is readily available through local human service agencies and the census bureau.

We also need to identify the spiritual assets of our community —the number of faith communities and believers. Together, these two research pieces give us a picture of our "mission field" and our "mission force." Armed with accurate information, we can determine best how to go forward.

In 1994, twenty-one-year-old Pastor Matthew Barnett began the Los Angeles "Dream Center" by walking around his neighborhood looking for unmet needs. He saw the thousands of outcast people living on the fringes of society. Today the Dream Center— "the church that never sleeps" has adopted fifty city blocks (twenty-one hundred homes!) that it serves with two hundred volunteer staff.

Its Franciscan Hospital campus houses four hundred people in its rehab and discipleship program and feeds more than twenty-five thousand people a week. They have a free 24-hour medical clinic, a mobile medical unit, and dozens of effective ministries that are finding needs and meeting them. Scores of churches around our country have adopted the Adopt a Block strategy as a means of touching the lives of people around them.

In our town of Boulder, Colorado, the pastors realized that they knew very little about the other agencies that were serving our community. They decided to organize a one day "Magic Bus Tour" to meet with the directors of these agencies, to find out what they did and what help they needed. They visited the local shelter, the food bank, a day-care facility, a health clinic, a home for runaway youth, the AIDS project, and more—a total of eight agencies. It was the beginning of bridge-building relationships between the faith community and the community where new openness, healing and friendships have begun.

Our pastors are now ministering to AIDS patients and utilizing their churches for overflow nights in partnership with the home-less shelter. One pastor, who is now taking meals to AIDS patients on a weekly basis, was drawn into this ministry by two things: "This was a group of people who were in need of the grace of God and also the group I was most uncomfortable with, so I just thought it was something God wanted me to be a part of. If any-thing, this ministry is changing my life."

10 *From teacher to learner.*
   "Everyone should be quick to listen, slow to speak"
   (James 1:19).

It is interesting to note that for the historic African-American churches, the concept of holistic ministry is not a new concept. They have never suffered from trying to split effective evangelism from social justice or meeting the needs of those around them. It's how they've always done church.

A study of 2,150 black churches by C. Eric Lincoln and Lawrence H. Mamiya, in their book *The Black Church in the African American Experience*, reported that nearly 70 percent "of black churches are involved with social service agencies and non-church programs in dealing with community problems."

The effective churches see the community as one that is full of assets more than full of problems. Churches in New York City such as Concord Baptist Church of Christ, Allen AME, Bethel Gospel Assembly, and those in Los Angeles like First AME, Faithful Central Bible Church, and West Angeles COGIC have led the way in transforming and preserving their communities. John DiIulio, former director of the White House Office of Faith-Based and Community Initiatives, cites a study of over four hundred of the roughly two thousand community-serving congregations in Philadelphia:

▲ Over 90 percent of urban congregations provide social services, from preschools to prison ministries, from food pantries to health clinics, from literacy programs to day-care centers, etc.

▲ The replacement value of their services in Philadelphia alone is a very conservatively estimated quarter-billion dollars a year.

Suburban congregations have much to learn from these innovative leaders and ministries.

Where do we go from here?

From Isaiah 65:17-25 Ray Bakke outlined seven characteristics of a healthy community from the heart of God:

▲ Public celebration and happiness (vv. 18, 19)
▲ Public health for children and the aged (v. 20)
▲ Housing for all (v. 21)
▲ Food for all (v. 22)
▲ Meaningful work (vv. 22, 23)
▲ Family support systems (v. 23)
▲ Absence of violence (v. 25)

This list outlines our potential marching orders. The Spirit of God is at work. There is a good chance that the next great movement of God will involve putting the Church back into community where it can be the leaven, salt, and light God designed it to be. Will we join God in this transforming work? For the sake of the gospel, the Church, and our communities, in faith—let's move forward!

If it falls to your lot to be a street sweeper, sweep streets like Michelangelo carved marble. Sweep streets as Shakespeare wrote pictures. Sweep streets so well that all the hosts of heaven will have to say, "Here lives the street sweeper who did his job well."

MARTIN LUTHER KING

What are the next steps for you?

▲ Which paradigms do you readily identify with? Which principles or illustrations speak to you most strongly?

▲ How would you answer the question, "Tell me about the impact your church is having on your community?"

▲ Define your "growth model" for individuals? Can those in your church grow significantly apart from service? Why or why not?

▲ What are some natural ways you can begin building bridges into your community?
  • Where is the "low-hanging fruit" for your church?
  • Where do you sense is your first (or next) entry point into your community?
  • What are the internal/external barriers to entering into the life of your community

▲ What human service agencies would make natural "partner ministries" for your church

▲ How can you begin expressing "unity of purpose" with others in the faith community

▲ What are some ways that you can "bless" your city?

▲ How can you begin to get good information about your community's "mission field" and "mission force?"

▲ Discuss the "Ten Paradigm Shifts" with your staff/board at your next leadership retreat.[5]

WILL THE WORKPLACE MOVEMENT BECOME A TIPPING POINT?

Malcolm Gladwell has written a book called *The Tipping Point*. A "tipping point" is how an idea becomes an epidemic. It can take place when a product sells more products, a trend becomes a movement, or when social issues or religious movements spread just like viruses.

Consider a few events that led to "tipping points" in our society:

Martin Luther King—He started a movement around equal rights that became a tipping point that changed a long-held view of the separation of races. (William Wilberforce was the man in England who became the catalyst for the abolishment of slavery.)

Roe vs. Wade—This Supreme Court case made abortion legal in the United States in the '60s. It became a tipping point in our society.

Prayer in Public Schools—The abolishment of prayer in public schools in the '60s became another tipping point in America that has led to a steady decline in morality and family values.

TIPPING POINTS IN CHRISTIAN MOVEMENTS

In 1857 Jeremiah Lanphier began a prayer meeting on Wall Street in New York City, and within six months thirty thousand people were meeting for prayer. It became a major revival in America. More than one million people came to Christ. This was a tipping point in our nation.

Promise Keepers was a movement among men that began more than ten years ago. Stadiums of men repented of failing to provide spiritual leadership in their families. However, this movement has not tipped society to an epidemic of societal transformation.

Many people have become Christians through the preaching ministry of Billy Graham. However, has this led to a tipping point in our society? George Barna, a Christian researcher who has been tracking the growth of the Christian church in America has found that for more than ten years the percentage of those who claim to be "born again" has remained consistently at a 35 to 40 percent mark, and church attendance has declined. There has not been a tipping point that resulted from these movements.

BOOKS AND MOVIES THAT HAVE CROSSED TIPPING POINTS

There have been tipping points in Christian publishing. The *Left Behind* series is the best-selling Christian fiction series of all time. Millions of these books have been sold. The *Prayer of Jabez* and the *Purpose Driven Life* have broken publishing records and become best-sellers on secular book lists as well. However, have these breakthroughs led to a tipping point in society? No. None of these have tipped society to an epidemic in behavioral change.

The Passion of the Christ—Mel Gibson has generated a tipping point in movie history. His movie about the last twelve hours of the life of Christ has broken movie records and broken every rule in the book about what is required to make a Hollywood block-buster movie. His movie had subtitles and was spoken in an ancient language not spoken today. It became a movie for Christians to rally around. Will it become a tipping point or just another fad? Will more movies be created for theatre-goers who will attend Christian-content films?

NEGATIVE TIPPING POINTS IN AMERICAN SOCIETY

Following are some recent issues that could lead to tipping points in our society:

Janet Jackson—Her Super Bowl PR stunt in January 2004 led to a crackdown on indecency in the media. She lost a major movie role and her career may be severely impacted. People like Howard Stern, who has become the poster child of indecency for television and radio, was shut down by Clear Channel, a major media distributor who carried his program. Other radio shows have taken notice and have begun to clean up their acts. The FCC has increased their fines dramatically to hold the media more accountable.

Will the Jackson event lead to a greater acceptance of indecency, or will it lead to greater controls and a return to decency in the media? Only time will tell, but it is unlikely there will be a return to decency in the media without a heart change of some kind, one that would provide the motivation for permanent change.

Gay Marriage Act—For the first time in our society the question of whether a man and a woman should constitute the definition of marriage is being debated. How is this possible in a "Christian" nation? When the church becomes a passive voice, it no longer acts as salt and light.

Terrorism—Terrorism is changing the way we live. Americans are no longer safe on their own soil. Terrorism is costing our nation billions of dollars to insure its citizens' safety. It is causing Americans to think differently about homeland security. What tipping point might this lead to?

CHANGING THE 80/20 RULE IN THE 9 TO 5 WINDOW

Dr. Peter Wagner has said that the workplace movement has the potential to be as significant as the Protestant Reformation because it reaches those in society who have the power to make changes in society.

The 80/20 rule says that 80 percent of the activity will be achieved by 20 percent of the people, for example:

▲ 20 percent of criminals do 80 percent of the crime.

▲ 20 percent of motorists cause 80 percent of the accidents.

▲ 20 percent of beer drinkers drink 80 percent of the beer.

▲ 20 percent of Christians do 80 percent of the ministry activity.[1]

The workplace movement is about changing the 80/20 rule among believers in the 9 to 5 Window—the workplace. In an epidemic a tiny percentage of people do the majority of the work. Will the workplace movement be just another fad, or will it lead to a tipping point in our society?

Dr. Peter Wagner has said that the workplace movement has the potential to be as significant as the Protestant Reformation because it reaches those in society who have the power to make changes in society. When people in government, entertainment, education, military, and business begin to operate from a Christian worldview, we begin to see changes in laws and decisions that rule our nation. Church leaders have the ability to impact those who serve in these arenas.

Four Types of Christians in the Workplace

Ed Silvoso, author of *Anointed for Business*, observed that we have four types of Christians in the workplace today. The first type is a "survivor." Survivors have no positive impact for Christ in their workplaces. They are there to collect a paycheck and they "check their faith at the door" on Monday mornings. They have no purpose in their work lives.

The second type is one who lives by Christian principles. This may sound okay, but God calls us to a higher level; God has called us to a relationship with Him, not to principles alone.

The third type of Christian in the workplace is one who lives by the power of the Holy Spirit. He seeks God for direction in his work life and is led by God in his decisions.

Finally, the fourth type is the Christian who transforms his workplace for Christ. This is really the fruit of level three, or the third type.

Jeremiah Lanphier

As mentioned previously, in 1857 Jeremiah Lanphier became a transformer in his workplace, which led to societal transformation. A pastor in the small farming community of Almolonga, Guatemala, also became a transformer in his city.

Almolonga is a town of only twenty thousand people. Twenty years ago, this city was one of the worst in the nation. The poverty, violence, and spirit worship resulted in a people and community that were spiritually and physically bankrupt. There were four jails in the city, and alcohol and drug abuse were rampant. Almolonga was located in a farming area that depended upon produce sales for the primary source of income. During this period, the land was so arid that it yielded only four truckloads of produce a month.

There was a pastor in the city that began to pray and to fast with other intercessors three or four times a week. Over a period of time many people were saved. Lives began to change. The intercessors prayed against the spirit worship that had so impacted this city. As more and more people were changed by the power of the gospel, seeds of new life were planted in the city. Negative influences were overcome. There were miracle stories of healings and other extraordinary happenings reported. People were interested to know more because of the change they saw in their friends.

Now, twenty years later, the community of Almolonga is a transformed model city. Pastors and other Christian leaders pray together and fast three or four times a week, and 80 percent of the town are born-again Christians. The jails have now closed because of the lack of crime in the city. There are now two dozen evangelical churches in and God is even touching the agricultural community in a very unusual and miraculous way. They were only delivering four truckloads of produce a month, and now they are delivering forty truckloads a week—a 1,000 percent increase!

However, that is not the most remarkable thing. The produce they are harvesting is many times larger than the size of normal produce. Beets are four pounds, lettuce is the size of basketballs, and carrots are the size of a man's arm. If I had not seen it on video with my own eyes, I would not have believed it! Farmers pay cash for Mercedes trucks and place Christian names on their trucks. This community is sold out for Christ, and Christ seems to be sold out for them in every way. This is what I mean by the Kingdom of God being manifested in a physical way.

This is not the only community that has experienced such a transformation by God. The Sentinel Group, a ministry in Lynnwood, Washington, has done three one-hour video documentaries on different communities, one of which is Almolonga. However, the good news is there are more and more cities being transformed around the world.

John Wesley Became a Tipping Point

In the 1780s Methodism was birthed through John Wesley. He went from twenty thousand followers to ninety thousand in five years. Wesley was not the most charismatic preacher of his day when compared to John Whitefield. Nor was he considered the most knowledgeable theologian. Martin Luther and John Calvin were recognized as the leading theologians. His real genius was organizational.

When he preached in a city he stayed for a few days to form small groups of the most enthusiastic of his followers. He required them to attend weekly meetings and meet a strict code of conduct. This created a community around his beliefs in order to practice those beliefs in the context of daily life. This is why he was successful. He took teaching and made it relevant for those who were the most committed. This led to a tipping point and the formation of a major Christian denomination.

According to Malcom Gladwell in *Tipping Point*, there are three key types of people needed for an idea to become a tipping point.

THREE TYPES OF PEOPLE WHO ARE CATALYSTS FOR TIPPING POINTS

The Connector

The first type of person is the "Connector." These are people with a special gift for bringing the world together through networking. They have an extraordinary knack for making friends and acquaintances. They know a lot of people. The kinds of people they know are an important aspect of their ability to have an impact. They are connected to different worlds and can bring them all together to affect change. They have an uncanny ability to be at the center of events. Word of mouth epidemics are the work of Connectors.

The Mavens

The second group of people is the "Mavens" which is Yiddish that means "one who accumulates knowledge." These people are passive collectors of information. They are information brokers who like to get information and share it with others. They connect people to the marketplace and have the inside scoop on the marketplace. They are socially motivated and want to solve their own problems by solving other people's problems. They tend to be unselfish and have a motivation to serve others without an agenda other than to help. The difference between a Connector and Maven is that a Connector will tell ten friends where to stay in L.A. and five will take his advice. A Maven will tell ten and all ten will stay there.[2] Both have the power to start word-of-mouth epidemics.

The Salesman

Ultimately someone must be persuaded to take action. Mavens are not persuaders as much as information brokers. They won't twist your arm. Mavens provide the message. Connectors are social glue. But it is the "Salesman" who completes the triangle of relationships that lead to epidemics. He has the ability to persuade when we are unconvinced of what we are hearing through the Connector or Maven. They are critical to the tipping point of word-of-mouth epidemics.

Most pastors exhibit all three of these attributes. They are connectors: they know lots of people. They are mavens: they have knowledge of the subject matter. And they are salesmen: they are persuasive in delivering a message. This makes a powerful combination that can begin an epidemic. So what's the problem? Church leaders have not bought into the understanding of what it really means to equip and commission workplace believers into the marketplace as a mission field.

When church leaders teach workplace believers that their faith life can be integrated into their work life it has the ability to begin an epidemic. Believers have not understood how to do this in a way that does not jeopardize their jobs. They have not understood how to apply the Word of God to daily work life situations. They need it broken down by the pastor so they can apply it to relevant situations.

MOVEMENT PROGRESSIONS— INNOVATORS TO LAGGARDS

Everett M. Rogers developed a measurement called Movement Progression that defines how people integrate technology into their lives. Five distinct stages involve five distinct types of people before anything new will be embraced that will ultimately reach the masses.

When a technological innovation is introduced, not everyone adopts it at the same moment. Rather, there will be innovators (the first users) and there will also be laggards (the last users) and several in between. Based upon the examination of a large number of studies in innovation diffusion, Rogers proposed a method of adopter categorization.

First, it was observed that the time to adoption follows the bell-shaped Gaussian curve when the frequency histogram is plotted against time. In turn, this meant that the cumulative number of adopters follows an S-shaped curve. Rogers suggested that the normal curve be discretized as follows:

- ▲ The first 2.5 percent of the adopters are the "innovators."
- ▲ The next 13.5 percent of the adopters are the "early adopters."
- ▲ The next 34 percent of the adopters are the "early majority."
- ▲ The next 34 percent of the adopters are the "late majority."
- ▲ The last 16 percent of the adopters are the "laggards." [3]

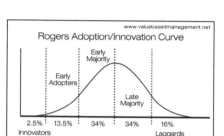

The innovation adoption curve of Rogers is a model that classifies adopters of innovations into various categories, based on the idea that certain individuals are inevitably more open to adaptation than others.

Innovators: Brave people, pulling the change. Innovators are very important in communication.

Early Adopters: Respectable people, opinion leaders, try out new ideas, but in a careful way.

Early Majority: Thoughtful people, careful but accepting change more quickly than the average.

Late Majority: Skeptical people, will use new ideas or products only when the majority is using it.

Laggards: Traditional people, caring for the "old ways," are critical toward new ideas and will only accept it if the new idea has become mainstream or even tradition.

I believe we are in the Innovator to Early Adopter stage in the workplace movement. These are the Joshua and Calebs in the Church. They do not fear the giants but want to conquer them.

They like the fight! The 2.5 percent of innovators are those who have been involved in workplace ministry for many years or business leaders who have been living out their faith in the workplace. They have been in the trenches and now see early adopters embracing the message.

The early adopters include major leaders in the body of Christ who have not been previously involved in the workplace movement but are now making a commitment to it. These include:

- ▲ Dr. Peter Wagner, Global Harvest Ministries and Wagner Leadership Institute

- ▲ Ed Silvoso, Harvest Evangelism

- ▲ Dr. Bob Reccord, North American Mission Board of the Southern Baptist Denomination

- ▲ Billy Graham Evangelistic Association

- ▲ John Maxwell, Injoy Group

- ▲ Promise Keepers

- ▲ A select group of major churches throughout the United States

In addition to these major leaders, God is raising up new ministries at the grass root level. Twelve years ago we could only identify about twenty-five formalized workplace ministries. Today we have identified more than twelve hundred non-profit workplace ministries, colleges, and churches that are making faith at work a primary focus of their agenda.[4]

In order for the workplace movement to become an epidemic, we will need to see the movement transition to the early majority and late majority stages. At this point the movement will have an impact on society and for the first time begin to see cities transformed in society.

Elk River, Minnesota, is a good example of this. Chuck Ripka is a banker in Elk River, a town of about 20,000. In the first twelve months of operation of his new bank, Chuck saw fifty salvations and forty physical healings inside the bank. The bank is far ahead of its financial projections of $16 million as a first year goal to realizing $50 million in actual deposits. Chuck holds prayer meetings for customers in the boardroom, serves as a catalyst to bring church leaders and workplace leaders together in the city, and has begun prayer walks in the schools. The mayor and other leaders in the community are Christians who are making an impact on their city. Elk River may be the first city transformed in our nation!

If we are to see the workplace movement become more than a fad, we will need workplace and church leaders to capture the vision and become the Joshuas and Calebs of our day. They must spy out the land and then take possession of it.

Wouldn't it be great to be the generation that becomes the catalyst for real transformation of our society?

The Spirit of God is speaking to the Church today. We are each called to bring the Kingdom of God into all spheres of life so that we can truly agree with Jesus' prayer:

> *Our Father in heaven, hallowed be your name,*
> *your kingdom come, your will be done* on earth as it is in heaven.
> *Give us today our daily bread. Forgive us our debts,*
> *as we also have forgiven our debtors.*
> *And lead us not into temptation, but deliver us from the evil one.*
> (Matt. 6:9-13, emphasis mine)

WORKPLACE MINISTRY Q&A
(If you only have ten minutes, read this!)

How would you define workplace ministry? Workplace ministry is the intentional focus of equipping men and women in *all* spheres of work and society to understand and experience their work and life as a holy calling from God. It is a movement designed to establish the church in the 9 to 5 Window and to change the 80/20 rule from 20 percent of people doing ministry to 80 percent.

Is workplace ministry an evangelism program? Not in the sense of how most people think about evangelism. Workplace ministry is a holistic approach to bringing Christ into our work lives. When we do this, all aspects of life and work are impacted. Associates at work become the primary source of building meaningful relationships that can lead to salvation. However, we must go beyond that.

We must allow God to show us how to work well, how to gain ideas and strategies to succeed, how to love our fellow workers, how to experience the power of God in a workplace context so that they see a difference in us. That is what changes the world. Workplace ministry is all about the priesthood of the believer. Evangelism is the fruit of workplace transformation. When people come to understand their totality in Christ—which includes work—the fruit is hearing God's voice, seeing miracles in their workplace, people coming to Christ, and a whole lot more.

Is workplace ministry part of most local church ministry today? No. Consider this statement by Doug Sherman, author of *Your Work Matters to God:* "Our surveys reveal that 90 to 97

SOME QUICK ANSWERS TO THE MOST COMMONLY ASKED QUESTIONS.

141

percent of Christians have never heard a sermon relating biblical principles to their work life." Most church members have never been *intentionally* trained to apply their faith in their work life where they spend 60 to 70 percent of their waking hours. When a survey is asked of the average congregation, "How many of you have been intentionally trained to apply your faith in your work life, very few hands are raised. Church leaders are often surprised because they feel they are equipping their people. The disconnect is because the teaching they receive is often not relevant to the level of application most Christians desire and need.

What is the best model in the Scriptures of workplace ministry? Jesus is our best model. He spent more than 50 percent of his life as a carpenter. Of 132 public appearances in the New Testament, 122 were in the workplace; of 52 parables He told, 45 had a workplace context. Of 40 divine encounters in the book of Acts, 39 were in the workplace. That is where most ministry took place. It wasn't in the synagogue.

More than 75 percent of the characters in the Bible were working people who did ministry as part of their work. Work in its different forms is mentioned more than 800 times in the Bible—more than all the words used to express worship, music, praise, and singing combined.

Should workplace ministry be another ministry like men's ministry? No. Workplace ministry is simply returning to the early foundations of the church that focused on equipping every believer to be a minister where they are. It is the priesthood of every believer.

However, in the early 300s the Greeks began to create the sacred/secular divide and pluralism came into the faith. This created a spiritual hierarchy that God never intended. Workplace ministry should be part of the DNA of every church. It should be the core message that affects all other areas. If it becomes just another program only those who are executives will participate. Workplace ministry is for moms, students, executives, secretaries, government workers, nurses, vocational ministry workers, and so forth. We all work. We all need to learn what it means to take Christ's presence into our workplace.

In what ways is the local church failing to do this?

▲ There is an unspoken word that says workplace believers are second class citizens spiritually by the words and actions often communicated in our churches. It is a sin of omission. When we use terms like "I am in full-time Christian work" it alienates those in secular work.

▲ When we commission missionaries in public services without ever commissioning workplace believers as having equal importance, we are sending a message to the average Christian that his ministry at work is simply less spiritual and not as important as the work of the overseas missionary.

▲ When we view workplace believers primarily for their monetary contributions we are validating them for only one purpose.

▲ When we equate ministry with their activity in the local church, we are saying the rest of the week at work is not ministry.

There are many other ways we alienate the average worker.

Isn't men's ministry considered another form of workplace ministry? No. In fact, most men's ministry does not address this important area and in my opinion has been a major oversight of men's ministry today. "If Christ is not Lord of my work, He will never be Lord of my family," said Doug Sherman, author of *Your Work Matters to God*. I believe this quote from Doug is true because most men get a great deal of self-esteem needs from their work. If Christ is not part of that, I would agree He will not be a part of any other aspect of his life. This is why men's ministry would be wise to incorporate the importance of men experiencing Christ in their workplaces and resource them.

What can churches do to equip and release their people into their workplace as missionaries? We need to consider the workplace as the major "9 to 5 Window" for missions today. We thought we could change cities through pastors and church leaders and prayer walks. This is not true. Church leaders don't have the authority in the cities. We need to equip and affirm the apostles, prophets, teachers, evangelists, and pastors in the workplace.

We need to think about church planting in a different way: *How many churches can a local church plant in the workplace this year?* We need to think about building the kingdom of God in the workplaces in our cities—prayer groups, Bible studies, prayer breakfasts, outreach luncheons, and so on. We have a complete list of ideas for churches at *www.icwm.net*. And we can help direct churches to other ministries who specifically are working with churches as this new move of God is emerging.

> It has to be intentional, long term and foundational to the church. The pastor must totally buy into it.

How does the local church often fail to encourage workers to see that their work is on par with vocational ministry? We often commission overseas missionaries in a public ceremony. Just as Barnabas and Paul had hands laid on them and were commissioned, workplace believers need to be commissioned as missionaries to their spheres of influence. By failing to do this we are failing to validate their calling in their work-life area.

Finally, we need pastors to do what they are called to do—equip their people to be effective where they spend 60 to 70 percent of their waking hours—the workplace. In order to do this *it has to be intentional, long term and foundational to the church. The pastor must totally buy into it.*

PART 1:
SERMON IDEAS

You can begin to encourage the workplace believers in your congregation by teaching and preaching on the subject of work and calling. The Scriptures are loaded with wonderful illustrations of those in the workplace who were used to impact the Kingdom of God. Mark Greene, in his book *Supporting Christians at Work,* provided a good list of key topics:

Theology of work	Success	Pressure
Vocation	Failure	Time management
Ministry at work	Ambition	Flirting
Dealing with bosses	Leisure	Sexual temptation
Being in authority	Rest	Truth-telling
Creation	Sabbath	Green issues[1]
Spirituality at work		

Biographical sketches of biblical characters and their vocations and their spiritual impact are also great ways to develop sermon ideas around a workplace theme.

Biblical Texts Ideal for Sermon Development

Following are devotional concepts from my book *TGIF Today God Is First.* Each of these devotionals or stories provides texts for the development of sermon ideas. These are just a few to get you started.

Jesus was the model workplace believer. Please refer to our earlier references to Jesus and the facts surrounding His ministry in the workplace.

Dissolving Partnerships

Abraham and Lot had to split up. Abraham chose to yield to Lot and took the weaker position. He went to Mamre, the "place of strength." Genesis 13:18

One day Abraham and his nephew Lot realized that the land they were living on could no longer support both families and all their flocks. It was decision time. They were going to have to split up. This meant someone had to go a different direction. But who should get first choice of the land? Obviously, Abraham was Lot's senior and by all rights should have that choice. Abraham could have pulled rank on Lot since he was the elder. This story is the model for splitting a business partnership. However, few workplace believers are willing to follow Abraham's example.

Abraham took a totally different approach to solving this problem. He told Lot to choose which land he wanted. Imagine, Abraham could have been dooming himself and his family if he was unable to find adequate land and water for them. He gave up his rights in the matter, and Lot took full advantage. "Lot looked up and saw that the whole plain of the Jordan was well watered, like the garden of the Lord, like the land of Egypt, toward Zoar" (Gen. 13:10). So Lot left and took up residence in the valley later to be known as Sodom and Gomorrah. Sometimes what seems good on the front end turns out to be disastrous later. Such would be the case for Lot and his family.

As for Abraham, he made a choice. He decided to take life's high road—a choice that didn't necessarily mean his life circumstances would benefit him. He was willing to leave that outcome to God. He made the decision based on an eternal measuring stick. Interestingly, the place where Abraham moved was called Mamre. In Hebrew, the name Mamre means "strength." How can choosing the weakest position become "strength"? Jesus must have asked the same question of His Father when faced with the proposition of going to the cross. How can the cross be a place of strength? The devil thought he had won, but the cross is what freed the captives for eternity. The Bible tells us that when we are weak, then we are really strong. To willingly choose the way of the cross becomes our strength.

Getting Promoted

God is the promoter of people. We need not promote ourselves. Proverbs 27:2

Many years of owning and operating an ad agency taught me that positioning was defined as a place or position that a product, service, or person held in the mind of the audience. We knew that often perception was reality for people, regardless of the truth. For years, I spent time and money seeking to position our company in the minds of our prospective clients. Although it would seem that is a natural and logical marketing function, I later discovered there is a dangerous flaw when we attempt to position ourselves by promoting our own attributes. I discovered that positioning is a by-product of who we are and what we do, not an end in itself.

King David was my first biblical lesson in coming to understand the difference. Here was a man who had committed adultery and murder, and failed many times in his family life. Yet, God describes David as a "man after God's own heart." Isn't that interesting? Why would God describe someone who had obviously failed in many areas as one who was after God's own heart? Throughout David's life, we find frequent descriptions made by God: 'so David's fame spread throughout every land...." (1 Chron. 14:17). Although David did make many mistakes, his heart was soft toward God and sought to praise Him. David wrote the majority of the Psalms. God honored what was in David's heart, not his perfection. I believe that God's strategic placement of David was so that we may learn from and be drawn to the attribute of David that God primarily wanted him known for—a heart bent toward Him. His positioning was a by-product of who he was, not an end in itself. In our business and personal life, our positioning among those who will know us should be a by-product of our life and service, not an end itself.

What is your "position" today among your peers? I once asked my Bible study group to ask others, "What do you think of when someone mentions my name?" This exercise can bring some interesting revelations. It might motivate us to make some changes, or it might confirm that God is doing a great work in you.

Understanding Our Call

John the Baptist understood his role in life to prepare the way for Jesus. Each of us must understand our roles.
John 3:27

"God never gave you that property," said my friend who had entered my life at a time of great turmoil. These were hard words at the time. I was separated in my marriage, and my financial resources were drying up on all fronts. It was like rowing a boat with five big holes in it, not knowing which one to try to plug. My business, my personal finances, my marriage, all seemed to be drying up at the same time. My friend had made an observation about some land we had purchased years before. His point was that I had acquired something that God had never given me. In other words, it was not a Spirit-directed purchase that was blessed by God. It was not a by-product of God's blessing; it was a source of sweat and toil born out of the wrong motives of the heart.

When John's disciples came to him and asked if he was the Messiah, he responded that he was not and that one could only be what God had given him to be. He was a forerunner to the Messiah, and he was fulfilling a call God had given him. We cannot acquire and become anything that God has not given us. God gave John that anointing. We must ask whether we are trying to be or trying to acquire anything God has not given us. When we seek to acquire anything that God has not given us, we can expect God to respond to us like any good father would to a child. He will remove that which the child is not supposed to have.

David understood this principle. When he was preparing to furnish the temple, he told God in his prayer, "Everything comes from You, and we have given You only what comes from Your hand" (1 Chron. 29:14b).

Blessing Those Who Curse You

Taking the high road when we are persecuted is often a test from God. 2 Samuel 16:11-12

As David's enemies were increasing and he was fleeing the city from his son who was seeking to take his throne, a man named Shimei began heaving rocks and cursing him as he passed by. Cursing the king was against the law, so David had every right to cut off the man's head—as his generals were encouraging him to do. Here we see the difference between Saul and David in their response to those who would seek to do them harm. This is the defining difference between a leader who seeks to lead through a vertical dimension with God versus a horizontal fix-it mode. God knew David as a man after His own heart. Yet, David was a murderer, adulterer, and had failed in many areas of his life. But one thing separated this leader from all the rest: He had a heart that sought to please God and be in His will. When David blew it, he repented.

What is the purpose God desires to accomplish with the estranged relationship you may have with someone? Has He brought this affront to find out what is in your heart today? Will you seek revenge and solve the problem yourself? Or will you find the grace to allow God to carry out vengeance in His time if it is needed? When I learned this lesson to stay vertical with God and avoid the trap of fixing things in my own energies, it was a day of freedom. No longer was it my problem. We must examine our own heart in these matters. But if we are clean, then this affront is for character building. It is the only way God builds the deepest level of character in His saints. A. W. Tozer tells us, "It is doubtful whether God can bless a man greatly until he has hurt him deeply." God actually rises up storms of conflict in relationships at times in order to accomplish that deeper work in our character. We cannot love our enemies in our own strength. This is graduate-level grace. Are you willing to enter this school? Are you willing to take the test? If you pass, you can expect to be elevated to a new level in the Kingdom. For He brings us through these tests as preparation for greater use in the Kingdom. You must pass the test first.

It is doubtful whether God can bless a man greatly until he has hurt him deeply.

A. W. TOZER

God-Inspired Delays

God does not always move on our timetable. Such was
the case for Lazarus.
John 11:6

Delays in our life are not always easy to handle or to reconcile
in our minds. Often, when God does not answer our prayers in
the time that we feel He should, we appoint all sorts of characteristics to God's nature that imply He does not care. Such was the
case with Lazarus' sisters when Lazarus became ill and died. Jesus
was a close friend to Lazarus and his two sisters, Mary and
Martha. (Mary, you may recall, was the woman who came and
poured perfume on Jesus' feet.) When Jesus arrived two days later,
Martha shamed Him by saying, "If You had come he would not
have died." She implied that He didn't care enough to come when
sent for. It was a matter of priorities for Jesus, not lack of love.

God often has to delay His work in us in order to accomplish
something for His purposes that can be achieved only in the
delay. Jesus had to let Lazarus die in order for the miracle that was
about to take place to have its full effect. If Jesus had simply
healed a sick man, the impact of the miracle would not have been
as newsworthy as resurrecting a man who had been dead for four
days. This is Jesus' greatest "public relations act" of His whole
ministry. What many do not realize is that the key to the whole
story is in the next chapter.

Many people, because they had heard that He had given this
miraculous sign, went out to meet Him. So the Pharisees said to
one another, *"See, this is getting us nowhere. Look how the whole
world has gone after Him!"* (John 12:18-19).

If Jesus had not raised Lazarus from the dead, there would

have been no crowds to cheer the Lord when He came into Jerusalem riding on a donkey.

God often sets the stage so that His glory is revealed through the events that He orchestrates. He did this with Moses and Pharaoh, allowing delay after delay for release of the Israelites from Egypt. He did this with Abraham and Sarah for the promised child, Isaac. God granted Sarah a baby past the age of childbearing in order to demonstrate His power.

God did this in my own life. He delayed the fulfillment of what I believed He called me to do for several years. But the delays provided the necessary preparation and greater glory that God was to receive. My friend, don't take the delays lightly. Do not faint as God places you in what seems to be a holding pattern. God is at work. God knows the purposes for His delays. Don't give up, for they are for His greater glory; so we need to remain faithful.

Obedience-Based Decisions versus Skill and Ability

God calls us to obedience, not to reason and analyze.
1 Chronicles 14:15a

The Philistines were attacking. David wanted to know how to respond. His first inquiry of God revealed that he was to attack the Philistines straightaway and God would give him victory. David followed God's instruction and gained victory. Shortly after, the Philistines mounted another attack. *"So David inquired of God again, and God answered him, 'Do not go straight up, but circle around them and attack them in front of the balsam trees'"* (1 Chron. 14:14).

David was a well-trained warrior, a strategist. Yet, we find that David's dependence on God to direct his efforts was very great. In fact, after he won the first battle, he went right back to inquire again. This is the most important lesson we can learn from this story. God told David to attack, but only after he heard the marching in the balsam trees.

How many times have you or I operated in the workplace based only on our skill and ability, without seeking to know the details of God's will in the matter? David could have simply assumed that since he had won the last battle, surely God would give him victory the same way. No. David had learned that communicating with the living God is the only sure way of victory. His skill was not enough. He had to have God's blessing.

How many times have we worked in our work life the same way each time only because it was the way we did it last time? What if God has a better way? What if God has a different plan than ours? *"So David inquired of God ..."* These are the important words that we are to learn from. We must be in such relationship with God that we are constantly inquiring of His mind on every matter. When we do this, we can expect the same results that David achieved-success in our endeavor and recognition by God. *"So David's fame spread throughout every land, and the Lord made all the nations fear him"* (1 Chron. 14:17). This is the reward of obedience to God. We don't have to build a name for ourselves. God will see to it that we are honored for our obedience. He wants to make known those servants who are willing to obey Him at all costs.

The Skillful Worker

Bezalel was the first man described as being filled with the Spirit of God. He was a craftsman. Proverbs 22:29; Exodus 31:1-5

The Lord has called each of us to be excellent in what we do. Those whom God used in the Kingdom as workplace ministers were skilled and exemplified excellence in their field. Not only were these men skilled, they were filled with God's Spirit.

"Then the Lord said to Moses, 'See, I have chosen Bezalel son of Uri, the son of Hur, of the tribe of Judah, and I have filled him with the Spirit of God, with skill, ability and knowledge in all kinds of crafts—to make artistic designs for work in gold, silver and bronze, to cut and set stones, to work in wood, and to engage in all kinds of craftsmanship'" (Exodus 31:1-5).

Consider Huram, the master craftsman of bronze in whom Solomon entrusted much of the temple designs. He was a true master craftsman (see 1 Kings 7:14).

Consider Joseph, whose skill as an administrator was known throughout Egypt and the world. Consider Daniel, who served his king with great skill and integrity. The list could go on—David, Nehemiah, Aquila and Priscilla.

I recall the first issue of an international publication we began. It was common to hear the comment, "It doesn't even look like a Christian magazine." They were saying the quality and excellence exceeded what they equated to Christian work. What a shame. Has inferior quality become synonymous with Christian work?

May we strive for excellence in all that we do for the Master of the universe.

Whatever you do, work at it with all your heart, as working for the Lord, not for men, since you know that you will receive an inheritance from the Lord as a reward. It is the Lord Christ you are serving (Colossians 3:23-24).

Decision-making

Trust in the Lord with all your heart and lean not on your own understanding; in all your ways acknowledge him, and he will make your paths straight. Proverbs 3:5, 6

This is one of the most quoted verses in the Bible related to gaining wisdom and direction from God. Yet I have never heard one teaching on this passage that teaches what I believe the psalmist is really saying. The first part is pretty easy; we are to trust with all our heart. But the next part is not so clear. We are not to lean on our own understanding. If we are not to lean on our own understanding, on whose understanding are we to lean? God's!

Throughout the Old Testament we find that God set up structures by which those in authority made decisions. God has always set a principle whereby we are to seek Him in all our decisions, that He might truly make our decisions. In the Old Testament, the priest made decisions based on which way the Urim and Thummim fell inside his breastplate. The casting of lots was another means of allowing a decision to be left with God. Proverbs says, *The lot is cast into the lap, but its every decision is from the Lord"* (Prov. 16:33). Another means of making a decision was through the agreement of two or three. No one could be guilty of any crime without the witness of two or three. This was a biblical way of confirming a matter. Still another means of making a decision is through a multitude of counselors.

Given all these scenarios, what are we to gain from these examples? We are told in Jeremiah 17:9a, *The heart is deceitful above all things and beyond cure.* So what really protects each of us from the deceit of our own heart? I believe it is the combination of all the above. When we get to a place with God that our decisions are accountable to others, whether that be a wife, a board, or a few close friends who are committed to the same godly ideals, this is when we are protected from the deceit of our own heart. This is one of the hardest things to yield to God-the right to make our own decisions. Yet, it is the most elementary principle God requires of us to receive His blessing in our lives.

This principle took a long time for me to appropriate. However, today I can tell you I would never make a major decision without the counsel of others who are close to me. Relational accountability has become lost in our culture due to our hunger for independence. I have experienced too often the hardship that results from making decisions that God isn't behind. Walking in obedience is the only real freedom in Christ.

Striving versus Abiding

Unless the Lord builds the house, its builders labor in vain.
Psalm 127:1a

What does it mean for the Lord to build the house? It almost seems a contradiction when we consider that we might be the builders in this passage. God wants us to allow Him to build the house. He explains further:

Unless the Lord builds the house, its builders labor in vain. Unless the Lord watches over the city, the watchmen stand guard in vain. In vain you rise early and stay up late, toiling for food to eat— for He grants sleep to those He loves (Psalm 127:1-2).

God is telling us there is a way of working without striving. There is a way to conduct business without sweating and toiling for outcome. His warning to each of us is to avoid thinking that outcome is based on our sweat and toil. Outcome is based on obedience. That outcome is sometimes more than we deserve. Sometimes it is less than we hoped for. His desire for each of us is to see Him working in our daily work life. He wants us to avoid looking to our own effort to gain an outcome.

One day Jesus called out to Peter from the shore of the lake and suggested he throw his net on the other side of the boat. It was this simple act of obedience that yielded a tremendous catch that he would not have received unless he obeyed.

We are called to work; He is called to bring forth the fruit. He is the vine. We are the branches. Fruit comes forth naturally from a healthy tree.

Today, ask God to show you when you enter into striving. Ask Him to show you the difference between loving trust and obedience and striving for outcome. It can be challenging for us to balance this in our daily work experience. He wants to help us walk in this freedom and rest.

You Are Called to Live for a Cause Greater than Yourself

I can do everything through him who gives me strength.
Philippians 4:13

In the thirteenth century a man named William Wallace became the instrument of freedom from England's tyranny over Scotland. A very wicked king ruled England. A tragedy in the life of William Wallace launched him into living for this cause. Initially his cause was revenge, but soon his cause turned to something bigger than himself—freedom for a nation. When he challenged the commoners to fight for this freedom, they responded that the enemy was too great and that they might die on the battlefield. They also refused to fight for the nobles, the knights and leaders who had a vested interest in gaining more land for themselves versus a pure cause of freedom. Wallace's response: "Yes, we might die. We will all die sooner or later. But we will die for a cause worth dying for. So that our children and their children might live in freedom." This story was popularized in the movie Brave Heart (Sherman Oaks, California: Paramount Pictures, 1995).

Today we find many Christian workplace believers living a status quo relationship with God that is more characterized as "business as usual" than a life demonstrating God's power. Our focus is often more concerned with improving our standard of living than improving the Kingdom of God through our circle of influence. While this takes place, millions upon millions die without the saving grace of Christ. Many other Christians die never experiencing the freedom in Christ that His blood paid for. God has called each of us to live for a cause greater than ourselves—a life that is dependent on His grace and power to achieve things we never thought possible through our lives. This is His plan for your life. The apostle Paul prayed that He might experience the power of the resurrection in his life. This power is available to you and me to live for a cause greater than ourselves. Ask God what He wants to achieve through your life today. And consider yourself dead already to the consequences of what that might mean for you.

Faith versus Presumption

Faith is different from presumption. Do you know the difference? Genesis 16:2

Presumption is based on our own reasoning. Abraham and Sarah fell into presumption when they got too old to have children. God had promised a son to Abraham and Sarah—a son who would fulfill His promise to birth a nation. But Abraham and Sarah were past the normal age for childbearing. So, they concluded that God needed help to work out His plan.

Many workplace believers make the same mistake every day. We make assumptions about what we believe God is doing and wants us to do. However, before we really have full assurance that God has spoken to us on the matter and revealed His perfect action plan, we move forward with our steps to get it done. How do we protect ourselves from presumption? The Proverbs tell us that there is safety in a multitude of counselors (see Prov. 11:14 KJV). Submitting our decisions to others for confirmation protects each of us from the deceit of our own heart. This process will protect us from presumption and encourage us to move in faith. The next time you believe God is directing you toward a specific action, consult with your spouse first, then some close, spiritual friends who will take the time to prayerfully consider your request. If you don't have consensus, wait until you do before you move forward. God will move through this process to His desired will for the matter.

Confidence in Numbers

David placed too much faith in the size of his army.
2 Samuel 24:10

It just seems to be human nature. As we grow in wealth and ability, our confidence moves from complete trust in the Lord to trust in our resources. King David decided one day that he needed to know how many fighting men he had in his army. This was a grievous sin in the nation of Israel. God always made it clear to the nation that He, not their army, was their source. It was against the law of God to number the troops. David's general, Joab, knew the serious nature of such an action.

But Joab replied to the king, "May the Lord your God multiply the troops a hundred times over, and may the eyes of my lord the king see it. But why does my lord the king want to do such a thing?" (2 Samuel 24:3).

Joab knew that David was treading in dangerous waters when he brought up the idea to him. But David had it in his mind that this is what he was going to do. And he did. The result: God judged David for this sin by smiting the nation with a plague that resulted in the loss of 70,000 lives.

Recently, I was having lunch with a former stockbroker who lost everything in the 1987 stock crash in the United States. He made an interesting comment. "You cannot know how to fully trust the Lord in the financial area until you really have to. When I lost everything, I was forced to trust Him when I knew I could not pay my next bill unless God provided. This was the time I learned to trust God. I never had to trust God before I lost my money because I had plenty. We don't willingly enter this level of trust with God."

Ask God today to keep you from trusting in your own resources. Ask Him how to balance trust and blessing from Him this day.

Death and Birth of a Vision

Sometimes things must die before they can birth in the Spirit. John 12:24

Almost every significant thing God births He allows to die before the vision is fulfilled in His own way.

- ▲ Abraham had a vision of being the father of a great nation (birth). Sarah was barren and became too old to have children (death). God gave Abraham and Sarah a son in their old age. He became the father of a great nation (fulfillment).

- ▲ Joseph had a vision that he would be a great leader and that many would bow down to him (birth). Joseph's brothers sold him to some merchants and he became a slave. Later he was falsely condemned to spend his years in prison (death). God allowed Joseph to interpret the dreams of the butler and baker and later the king, whereupon, he was made a ruler in the land (fulfillment).

- ▲ Moses had a vision of leading his people out of the bondage of Egypt (birth). Pharaoh as well as his own people drove Moses out of Egypt after Moses' first attempt to relieve their bondage (death). God gave Moses signs and wonders to convince Pharaoh to free the people and bring them out of Egypt and into the Promised Land (fulfillment).

- ▲ The disciples had a vision of establishing the Kingdom of God with Jesus (birth). The very ones He came to save killed Jesus, and the disciples saw Him buried in a tomb (death). God raised Jesus from the dead, and the disciples performed great miracles until the gospel had spread through all the world (fulfillment).

- ▲ A grain of wheat has a "vision" of reproducing itself and many more grains of wheat (birth). The grain dies in the ground (death). A harvest springs up out of the very process of "death" in the ground (fulfillment).

Has God given you a vision that is yet unfulfilled? If that vision is born of God, He will raise it up in His own way. Do not try to raise the vision in your own strength. Like Moses, who tried to fulfill the vision of freeing the Hebrews by killing the Egyptian, it will only fail. But wait on your heavenly Father to fulfill the vision. Then you will know that it was His vision when He fulfills it in the way only He can do.

The Fallacy of Full-Time Christian Work

Whatever you do, work at it with all your heart, as working for the Lord, not for men, since you know that you will receive an inheritance from the Lord as a reward. It is the Lord Christ you are serving. Colossians 3:23, 24

"I didn't know you were in full-time Christian work," said my close friend as we were driving."I didn't realize that," she went on. I responded, "Every person who has followed the will of God in their life is in full-time Christian work." God calls some to the mission field, others to be accountants, and others to be advertising executives, and still others to be construction workers. God never made a distinction between sacred and secular. In fact, the

Hebrew word avodah is the root word having the same meaning of "work" and "worship." God sees our work as worship.

We have incorrectly elevated the roll of the Christian worker to be more holy and committed than the person who is serving in a more secular environment. Yet the call to the secular workplace is as important as any other calling. God has to have His people in every sphere of life. Otherwise, many would never come to know Him because they would be separated from society.

I learned this lesson personally when I sought to go into "full-time" service as a pastor in my late twenties, only to have God thrust me back into the business world unwillingly. This turned out to be the best thing He could have done for me, because it was never His will for me to be a pastor. He knew I was more suited for the workplace.

We are all in missions. Some are called to foreign lands. Some are called to the jungles of the workplace. Wherever you are called, serve the Lord in that place. Let Him demonstrate His power through your life so that others might experience Him through you today and see your vocation as worship to His glory.

Treasures in Darkness

Sometime God takes us to a depth of soul experience to reveal treasures in darkness. Isaiah 45:3

"I have never been in this place before. It is new ground for me, and I find I am way out of my comfort zone. I am scared to death to trust Him at this level. I had to confess to the Lord I have not been able to accept or believe His love for me in this area." Those were the words I expressed to a friend when I was in a difficult place in my life. That day when I confessed those words,

God led me to this passage of Scripture.

What we perceive as dark periods in our lives are designed to be treasures from God. They are actually riches stored in secret places. We cannot see those times in this light because of the often-accompanying pain or fear that prevents us from accepting these times as treasures. They have a particular purpose from God's viewpoint: "so that you may know that I am the Lord who summons you by name."

You see, unless we are cast into times in which we are completely at God's mercy for breakthroughs in our lives, we will never experience God's faithfulness in those areas. We will never know how personal He is, or that He can be trusted to meet the deepest needs in our lives. God wants each of us to know that we are "summoned by name." Every hair of our head is numbered. He knows every activity we are involved in. His love for you and me knows no bounds, and He will take every opportunity to demonstrate this to us.

Has God brought you into a place of darkness? Trust Him today to reveal that hidden treasure that can be found in this darkness. Let Him summon you by name.

Resolving the Ownership Issue

Who owns what we have? It is clear God owns it all.
Psalm 24:1-2

As Christian workplace believers, God calls us to view Him as the owner of everything. We are to be stewards of all that He entrusts to us. This is one of the hardest of all commandments to follow for the Christian workplace believer because, if we work hard at business, we receive all the benefits of that work. It appears as though all that we have achieved was through our hand. Yet God says that it is by His hand that we are able to make wealth (see Deut. 8). He is the source of that ability. As soon as we become owners and not managers, we fall into trouble with God.

Joseph understood that he was a steward of all the resources of Egypt. God promoted him to affect an entire region of the world. Joseph had more power, prestige, and wealth than any 30-year-old who ever lived before him. The temptation for him in this newfound role in life must have been great. Many a man has not been able to handle material success. Many of God's choicest servants began well in their calling and service to God only to fail at the end. Consider Hezekiah, the great king who achieved many great things but failed to acknowledge God's blessing at the end of his reign. His reign was cut short due to pride. Gideon's fate was similar. Success can lead to pride if we are not careful.

Planning for Success

God calls us to plan based on His leading. Jeremiah 10:23

In business I hear a lot about planning. Every January I hear workplace believers establishing their planning for the year. Corporations establish plans that cover anywhere from one to five years. Individuals establish personal life plans. There is only one problem that I see with most planning done by well-meaning believers. If God is not the originator and director of the plan, then that plan is doomed for failure. So often, Christian workplace believers set out to plan something that seems good in their own mind. The merits of what is being planned can look great, and it can even be a worthy endeavor. However, that is not the point. When Jesus said He came only to do the will of the Father, He could not consider doing anything that was not what the Father wanted, no matter how good or righteous it might appear to be.

"In his heart a man plans his course, but the Lord determines his steps" (Prov. 16:9). God must give us the vision for what He calls us to do. After we have the vision, we must ask Him if He wants us to take action on that vision and what the action steps entail. The Lord wants to direct each step of the planning process. David learned this lesson when he went to battle against his enemy, the Philistines. One day he inquired of God as to whether he was to go up against the Philistines, and the Lord said, *"Yes, but only when you hear the marching in the balsam trees."* It is a mistake to reason and analyze in order to come to a decision on a matter. The Lord already knows the answer. It is our responsibility to seek Him to find out His mind on the matter. Our planning must be established in Him. Only when we remain so connected to the source can we be assured of putting God's plan into place. Also, getting that plan confirmed through others will assure that we are not following the deceit of our own heart.

When you begin to plan next time, ask God for His wisdom for establishing the vision and action steps. You will be surprised how well He can plan.

The Profit Motive Is Not Always Evil
David considered the reward when fighting Goliath.
No taxes, a beautiful wife, and wealth were his rewards.
1 Samuel 17:26

You are called to a specific work. Jesus had a specific work to do. John 17:4

The Lord has revealed to us that the number one thing we are to do is love the Lord our God with all our heart and to love our neighbor as ourselves. His desire is for us to know Him and the power of His resurrection. These mandates deal with our relationship with Him. The fruit of this relationship must then result in our glorifying Him by completing the work He has given each of us to do. It will become a by-product of this relationship, not an end in itself.

What is the work God has called you to do? Jesus never did anything the Father had not instructed Him to do. He lived in such communion with the Father that He knew when to turn left and when to turn to the right. Is it possible to have such a relationship with our heavenly Father? I think that if it weren't, He would not have given us such an example.

"Call to Me and I will answer you and tell you great and unsearchable things you do not know" (Jer. 33:3). What has He called you to do? Perhaps you are called to be the best CPA in your city or the best advertising executive or the best office worker or assembly line person in your company. Whatever work He has called you to do, He will use you as His instrument to accomplish something that He has uniquely prepared you to do.

When our life is complete, what a glorious day it will be if we can each say, "I have completed the work You gave me to do." This will have brought great glory to Him.

To access these devotionals online go to: http://www.eprayerconnect.org/ Select **TGIF Today God Is First archives**. You may also find them on http://www.crosswalk.com. Click on devotionals.

To purchase the TGIF Today God Is First devotional book visit: www.faithandworkresources.com or call 678-455-6263 to order. There are 365 messages that provide an excellent resource for developing sermon ideas around. Only a few are listed here.

To subscribe to these devotionals free visit: http://www.freetgifsubscription.net. You can also receive our free e-book, *Faith & Work: Do They Mix?* when you subscribe.

PART 2:
BIOGRAPHIES OF WORKPLACE PEOPLE FOR SERMONS

Following are stories of individuals who have modeled their faith in their work lives. These are wonderful illustrations of workplace believers which will help people in your congregation apply faith in their vocations. Their stories are provided for you to use in sermons. They were excerpted from my devotional book, *TGIF*, published by Destiny Image Publishers.

Bezalel, a craftsman, designed the Ark of the Covenant, Exodus 31:1-5 (Also see devotional.)

Brigid of Ireland, social entrepreneur

Cyrus McCormick, retailer

D. L. Moody, shoe salesman

Eric Liddell, athlete turned missionary (Also see Chapter 5.)

George Müeller, founder of orphanage

George Washington Carver, inventor and farmer

Gideon, farmer turned reformer

J. C. Penney, retailer

R. G. LeTourneau, construction industry

Samuel Morse, inventor of technology

William Wallace, reformer (See devotional.)

Jeremiah Lanphier, stockbroker (Also see Chapter 6.)

Zerubbabel, politician

Daniel, government worker

Bezalel: Called to Craftsmanship

Bezalel was called by God to perform a most important work for Him. I am sure that Bezalel believed that he was naturally gifted with his hands to make fine crafts with gold, silver, and bronze. He probably did not associate it with God's work. But the Scripture tells us that God chose him and filled him with God's Spirit to enable him.

Does God call men and women into their vocations to fulfill His purposes—to fulfill that which needs to be accomplished throughout the world? Have you ever thought about how many occupations there are in the world? How did that balance of interest among each human throughout the world happen? Did it just happen? Was it by chance that we have only so many doctors, only so many accountants, only so many geologists?

Your interest in your vocation is not born of your own making. So many workplace believers and even pastors have made the mistake of encouraging us who have a deep desire to walk with Christ in the workplace to pursue vocational ministry. To remove us from the workplace where the greatest harvest is yet to occur would be to remove us from where God called us. Do not take this bait. Serve the Lord in the workplace where He has gifted you and called you.

I almost made this same mistake when God drew me to Himself when I was twenty-eight years old. I concluded that I must be called to be a pastor. I took steps to fulfill this by leaving my job and entering a Bible school for training. Upon completion, I took a job as an assistant pastor in a church. But God's mercy allowed me to be removed from that position only three months into it. I was "forced back into business," where God

Then the Lord said to Moses, "See, I have chosen Bezalel son of Uri, the son of Hur, of the tribe of Judah, and I have filled him with the Spirit of God, with skill, ability and knowledge in all kinds of crafts—to make artistic designs for work in gold, silver and bronze, to cut and set stones, to work in wood, and to engage in all kinds of craftsmanship."

Exodus 31:1-5

wanted me in the first place. It was a great lesson. I was never cut out to be a pastor in a church, but a "pastor" in the workplace.

Brigid of Ireland:
Living for a Cause Greater Than Yourself

If you were God and you wanted to send one of your servants to help the less fortunate in the world, how would you train your servant for this task? Our ways are not God's ways. We find an interesting story in the case of Brigid, a woman born in the early 400s in Ireland.

Brigid was born from a sexual encounter between an Irish king and one of his slaves. She was raised as a slave girl within the king's household and was required to perform hard work on the king's farm. From the beginning, Brigid took notice of the plight of the less fortunate. She would give the butter from the king's kitchen to working boys. She once gave the king's sword to a passing leper—an act that enraged the king. The king tried to marry her off, but to no avail. One day, Brigid fled the king's house and committed herself to belonging only to Christ.

Brigid sought other women who also wanted to belong only to Christ. Seven of them organized a community of nuns that became known as the settlement of Kildare, a place where many thatch-roofed dwellings were built, and where artist studios, workshops, guest chambers, a library, and a church evolved. These and other settlements became little industries all to themselves, producing some of the greatest craftsmanship in all of Europe.

Many of the poor had their lives bettered because of Brigid's ministry to them.

Brigid became a traveling evangelist, helping the poor and

preaching the gospel. When she died in 453, it is estimated that thirteen thousand people had escaped from slavery and poverty to Christian service and industry. Her name became synonymous with the plight of the poor. She was a woman who turned a life of slavery and defeat into a life lived for a cause greater than herself. She became a nationally known figure among her people, and the Irish people still recognize her each February 1.

God has called each of us to live for a cause greater than ourselves. If God asked you what you had done for the poor, what would you say? Jesus had a special place in His heart for the poor. Ask God how you might use your gifts and talents to improve the plight of the poor in your community.

Cyrus McCormick: Unlimited Potential

What might God want to accomplish through you in your lifetime? As a workplace believer, you may yet have your greatest contribution to society. Such was the case of Cyrus McCormick, born in 1809. Raised on a farm by an inventor father, Cyrus McCormick sought to invent a mechanical reaper to harvest wheat. His father's attempts at inventing a successful machine had failed until Cyrus, at twenty-two, created one that worked. McCormick had to overcome many setbacks including the loss of his patent fourteen years after his first invention. This opened up competition. Then, in 1837 he went bankrupt because of the bank panic of 1837. However, these setbacks did not prevent McCormick from achieving his goals.

He expanded his market by trying to sell his machine to European farmers in 1851. A long series of honors compensated for the lack of recognition and praise from his American compatriots.

I can do everything through Him who gives me strength.

Philippians 4:13

By 1856, he was not only a world figure but his factory produced more than four thousand reapers a year.

McCormick was a committed believer. He lived during the time of D. L. Moody and gave $10,000 to Moody to start the Chicago YMCA in 1869. That building burned along with his Chicago factory in 1871. By this time, McCormick was over sixty and wealthy enough to retire.

Before his death in 1884, he had given $100,000 to help open Moody Bible Institute. His son, Cyrus Jr., was to become the first chairman of the school's board. Cyrus McCormick was a devoted Christian who passed his faith on to his son who later met J. Pierpoint Morgan and became the first president of a combined reaper firm, the famed International Harvester Corporation. [John Woodbridge, ed., *More Than Conquerors*, (Chicago: Moody Press, 1992), 328-331.]

Jesus looked at them and said, "With man this is impossible, but with God all things are possible."

Matthew 19:26

D. L. Moody: A Shoe Salesman

Dwight L. Moody was a poorly educated, unordained, shoe salesman who felt God's call to preach the gospel. Early one morning he and some friends gathered in a hay field for a season of prayer, confession, and consecration. His friend Henry Varley said, "The world has yet to see what God can do with and for and through and in a man who is fully and wholly consecrated to Him."

Moody was deeply moved by these words. He later went to a meeting where Charles Spurgeon was speaking. In that meeting Moody recalled the words spoken by his friend, "The world has yet to see ... with and for and through and in ... a man!" *Varley meant any man! Varley didn't say he had to be educated, or brilliant, or anything else. Just a man! Well, by the Holy Spirit in him, he'd be one of those men.*

Then suddenly, in that high gallery, he saw something he'd never realized before. It was not Mr. Spurgeon, after all, who was doing that work; it was God. And if God could use Mr. Spurgeon, why should He not use the rest of us, and why should we not all just lay ourselves at the Master's feet and say to Him, "Send me! Use me!"?

D. L. Moody was an ordinary man who sought to be fully and wholly committed to Christ. God did extraordinary things through this ordinary man. Moody became one of the great evangelists of modern times. He founded a Bible college, Moody Bible Institute in Chicago, which sends out men and women trained in service for God.

Are you an ordinary man or woman in whom God wants to do extraordinary things? God desires that for every child of His. Ask God to do extraordinary things in your life. Begin today to trust Him to accomplish great things for His Kingdom through you.

Eric Liddell: Created for His Good Pleasure

Eric Liddell was an Olympic runner from Britain who won a gold medal in the 1924 Paris Olympics. He was a man who had a deep commitment to the Lord and had future plans of being a missionary. In the meantime, he knew God had given him a special gift to run, and he often said, "I feel God's pleasure when I run."

He spent years training for the Olympics. He passed each hurdle and qualified for the Olympics. Finally, the day came for him to run in the games that were held in Italy. There was only one problem. One of his running events was held on Sunday.

For we are God's workmanship, created in Christ Jesus to do good works, which God prepared in advance for us to do.

Ephesians 2:10

175

Liddell refused to run on Sunday, believing it dishonored the Lord's Sabbath. He held to his convictions and brought great persecution on himself. He made a decision that even if it meant losing his opportunity to compete, he would not run. God's laws were greater than man's applause. Just when the circumstances seemed hopeless, another situation arose that allowed Liddell to run on a different day.

So often this is the case in the spiritual realm. God tests our hearts to see if we will remain faithful to Him at the cost of something important to us. Once He knows where our loyalty lies, He opens a new door that meets the desires of our hearts.

God takes pleasure in seeing His creation used for His glory. Liddell understood why he was made to run; he used his gift of running to bring pleasure to his Creator. Later, Eric Liddell went on to serve God on the mission field.

Does your life work bring pleasure to the Lord? Do you understand that God instilled certain gifts and talents in you so that He might find pleasure in His creation of you? Take pleasure in the gifts God has given to you this day. And let His glory shine through you.

George Müeller: Sold Out

But whatever was to my profit I now consider loss for the sake of Christ.

Philippians 3:7

George Müeller was a man known for building orphanages by faith in the mid-1800s. He raised literally millions of dollars for his orphanages, yet died with little in his own bank account. When asked about his conversion experience he commented,

> I was converted in November of 1825, but I only came into the full surrender of the heart four years later, in July 1829. The love of money was gone, the love of place was

gone, the love of position was gone, and the love of worldly pleasures and engagements was gone. God, God alone became my portion. I found my all in Him; I wanted nothing else. And by the grace of God this has remained, and has made me a happy man, an exceedingly happy man, and it led me to care only about the things of God. I ask affectionately, my beloved brethren, have you fully surrendered the heart to God, or is there this thing or that thing with which you have taken up irrespective of God? I read a little of the scriptures before, but preferred other books; but since that time the revelation He has made of Himself has become unspeakably blessed to me, and I can say from my heart, God is an infinitely lovely Being. Oh, be not satisfied until in your own inmost soul you can say, God is an infinitely lovely Being!" [Basil Miller, *Man of Faith and Miracles*, (Minneapolis, Minnesota: Bethany House Publishers, n.d.)]

Many will never get to the place where George Müeller was in his spiritual life, because we are unwilling to release control of these areas of which he speaks. If we do release control, it usually is due to a process that God brings us through. Paul got knocked off a horse and was spoken to personally before he was willing to listen and follow completely. Peter had to live with Jesus three years and he still denied Him. It was only later, after he denied Jesus and realized how weak he was in his own faith, that he became fully committed to the Savior.

What will it take for you to fully surrender? You will know that you have given full surrender when power, money, and position no longer have meaning in your life. Paul said he came to a place where his life was the life of Christ only. It is a sacrificial life, but it is also a life of freedom, purpose, and meaning. Let God take full control and see His life lived fully through you.

George Washington Carver: Your Epitaph

What will be written on your epitaph? How do you want people to remember you? What type of legacy will your life leave behind?

I interviewed a very successful and powerful man one time for a magazine when this question came up. The man ran an international business that is a household name to all. He was a professed Christian, but he had difficulty answering my question. "I always knew someone would ask that question some day. I am not sure I am any more prepared to answer it now either," was the man's answer. He grappled for a few nice words, but it was clear he had not seriously considered his life much beyond his business success.

It is said of George Washington Carver that he got up early in the morning each day to walk alone and pray. He asked God how he was to spend his day and what He wanted to teach him that day. Carver grew up at the close of the Civil War in a one-room shanty on the home of Moses Carver—the man who owned his mother. The Ku Klux Klan had abducted him and his mother, selling her to new owners. He was later found and returned to his owner, but his mother was never seen again.

Carver grew up at the height of racial discrimination, yet he overcame all these obstacles to become one of the most influential men in the history of the United States. He made many discoveries with the use of peanuts and sweet potatoes. However, after he recommended farmers to plant peanuts and sweet potatoes instead of cotton, he was led into his greatest trial.

The farmers lost even more money due to the lack of market for peanuts and sweet potatoes. Carver cried out to the Lord, "Mr. Creator, why did You make the peanut?" Many years later, he shared that God led him back to his lab and worked with him to discover some three hundred marketable products from the peanut. Likewise, he made over one hundred discoveries from the sweet potato. These new products created a demand for peanuts and sweet potatoes, and they were major contributors to rejuvenating the Southern economy.

As he made new discoveries, he never became successful monetarily, but he overcame great rejection during his lifetime for being black. He was offered six-figure income opportunities from Henry Ford, and he became friends with presidents of his day, yet he knew what God had called him to do. His epitaph read: "He could have added fortune to fame, but caring for neither, he found happiness and honor in being helpful to the world." [John Woodbridge, *More Than Conquerors*, (Chicago: Moody Press, 1992), 312.]

Gideon:
A Farmer Turned into a "Mighty Warrior"

God always looks at His children for what they will be, not what they are now. The Lord already had seen Gideon as a leader of others, not just as a laborer who threshed wheat.

Gideon was an Israelite who lived during a time of oppression from the Midianites. God had allowed Israel to be oppressed because of their rebellion. However, the Israelites cried out to God, and He heard their cry for help. He decided to free them

"The Lord is with you, mighty warrior."

Judges 6:12

from the oppression of their enemies and chose a man with little experience in such matters to lead an army against Midian.

When God came to Gideon through a visit by an angel, the angel's first words to him were: *"The Lord is with you, mighty warrior."* God always looks at His children for what they will be, not what they are now. The Lord had already seen this man as a leader of others, not just a laborer who threshed wheat.

The apostle Paul said, *"I can do everything through Him who gives me strength"* (Phil. 4:13). God has reserved an inheritance for you and me. He has foreordained that we should accomplish great things in His name—not so that we will be accepted or become more valued, but to experience the reality of a living relationship with a God who wants to demonstrate His power through each of us.

What does God want to accomplish through you today? He used Gideon, with only three hundred men, to deliver Israel from an army of more than one hundred thousand. He demonstrated His power through one man who was willing to let God use what little faith he had to free a nation from oppression and bring glory to the God of Israel. The Lord delights in showing Himself strong through those who will trust Him.

The brother in humble circumstances ought to take pride in his high position.

James 1:9

J. C. Penney: Starting Over

Do you find yourself in humble circumstances? If so, James tells us that we are to take pride in this "high" position. These two things would seem to be an oxymoron. Most of us would not consider humble circumstances a high position. Successful business tells us that being on top means being wealthy, attaining favor and status, or having power to influence. However, Jesus influenced not from power, but from weakness.

J. C. Penney is a name synonymous with "department store." He first launched his chain of "The Golden Rule" stores in 1907. In 1910 his first wife died. Three years later, he incorporated as the J. C. Penney company. In 1923 his second wife died giving birth to his son. In 1929 the stock market crashed and he lost $40 million.

By 1932, he had to sell out to satisfy creditors. This left [Penney] virtually broke. Crushed in spirit from his loss and his health suddenly failing, Penney wound up in a Battle Creek, Michigan, sanitarium. One morning he heard the distant singing of employees who gathered to start the day with God: "Be not dismayed, whate'er betide, God will take care of you." Penney followed the music to its source and slipped into a back row. He left a short time later a changed man, his health and spirit renewed, and ready to start the long climb back at age fifty-six.

By 1951 there was a J. C. Penney store in every state, and for the first time sales surpassed $1 billion a year. [John Woodbridge, ed., *More Than Conquerors* (Chicago, Illinois: Moody Press, 1992), 340-343.]

The success of J.C. Penney can be traced to God's mercy in his life to bring him out of his humble circumstance. Do you find yourself in a humble circumstance? God is the only one who can help you see your humble circumstance from His viewpoint—a high position. It is a high position because of what God is going to teach you in this place. He does not intend you to stay there; it is merely a stopping place to learn some important things you would not learn otherwise. Press into God and trust Him for the outcome to your circumstances.

And David knew that the Lord had established him as king over Israel and that his kingdom had been highly exalted for the sake of His people Israel.

1 Chronicles 14:2

R. G. LeTourneau: Why God Blesses

King David learned an important lesson every leader must learn if he is to ensure God's continual blessing. He knew why God blessed him. It wasn't because he deserved it, though he was a man who sought God with his whole heart. It wasn't because of his great skill, though he was a great military strategist. It wasn't because he was perfect, for he committed some horrible sins during his reign as king. No, it was for none of these reasons. God blessed David for the "sake of His people Israel."

God never blesses an individual just for that person's exclusive benefit. God calls each of us to be a blessing to others. So often we forget this last part. R. G. LeTourneau, a businessman who built heavy construction equipment, came to realize this only after God took him through many trials. Once the Lord had all of LeTourneau, he came to realize that the question wasn't whether he gave 10 percent of what the Lord gave him. Rather, the question was, "What amount does He want me to keep?"

LeTourneau was known for giving 90 percent of his income toward the end of his career and was a great supporter of world missions. But the Lord doesn't bless workplace believers just for the ability to give financially. God has given workplace believers many more gifts beyond the financial. What is happening with the spiritual fruit of God's blessing on your life? Is it clogged, or is it freely flowing to others? Ask the Lord to free you to be a blessing to those in your circle of influence.

Samuel Morse: Our Plans and God's Plans

Have you ever heard of someone who spent years of preparation for one vocation only to end up doing something completely different? Perhaps this could be said of you. Quite often we have in our minds what we believe we want to do only to have a course correction. Often the course correction comes through a major crisis that forces us into an area that we would never have considered.

Such was the case for Samuel Morse. Born in 1791, Morse grew up desiring to be an artist, and he eventually became very talented and internationally known. However, it was difficult to make a living as an artist in America during that time. A series of crises further complicated his vocational desire when his wife died; then his mother and father also died soon after. He went to Europe to paint and reflect on his life. On his return trip aboard a ship, he was captivated by discussions at dinner about new experiments in electromagnetism. During that important occasion, Morse made the following comment, "If the presence of electricity can be made visible in any part of the circuit, I see no reason why intelligence may not be transmitted by electricity."

In the face of many difficulties and disappointments, he determinedly perfected a new invention, and, in 1837, applied for a patent that became what we know today as the telegraph. He also created Morse code. It was only later, after many more setbacks and disappointments, that his projects received funding. Samuel Morse later commented, "The only gleam of hope, and I cannot underrate it, is from confidence in God. When I look upward it calms any apprehension for the future, and I seem to hear a voice saying: 'If I clothe the lilies of the field, shall I not also clothe you?' Here is my strong confidence, and I will wait patiently

Many are the plans in a man's heart, but it is the Lord's purpose that prevails.

Proverbs 19:21

for the direction of Providence."

Morse went on to create several other inventions and can be recognized today as the father of faxes, modems, e-mail, the Internet and other electronic communication. ["Glimpses," Issue #99 (Worcester, Pennsylvania: Christian History Institute, 1998).]

God's plans may not always seem to follow our natural inclination. Perhaps God has you taking a path that may not lead to His ultimate destination for you. *Trust in the Lord, lean not on your own understanding, acknowledge Him in all you do, and He shall direct your path* (Prov. 3:5-6).

This was now the third time Jesus appeared to His disciples after He was raised from the dead.

John 21:14

William Wallace: Triumphant Defeats

William Wallace was a Scotsman who sought freedom from a tyrannical king of England in the 1200s. He initially took up this cause in retaliation for his own personal family losses. His cause grew among the people, and it became an insurrection against England. Wallace entreated Robert the Bruce, the future king of Scotland. However, Bruce betrayed Wallace in return for lands from the king of England. Wallace was turned over to the king of England to be tortured to death for crimes against England. Bruce realized his betrayal against Wallace and his own country. This remorse led to real repentance and a return to his commitment to the people of Scotland.

Wallace finally took ownership of the mission to free Scotland from England. He led the people of Scotland into subsequent battles against England and freed them. Wallace's defeat ultimately led to victory through Bruce. It took the lives of many, including Wallace, for victory to be accomplished. [James Mackay, *William Wallace, Brave Heart* (Edinburgh, Scotland: Mainstream Publishing, 1995).]

So often defeat is what is required before victory can be won. Jesus said that unless the seed dies and goes into the ground it cannot bring forth fruit (see John 12:24). The death of a vision is often required before the fulfillment can really take place. Have you failed at something in your life? Have you not seen the vision fulfilled you thought you were given? The vision may yet happen.

The disciples thought they suffered their greatest defeat when Jesus died on the cross. However, this defeat became the greatest victory on earth. Christ's death gave liberty. Forgiveness came to all men. New life came forth—new strength for the disciples. Resurrection and new life came as a result of a "defeat."

"There are triumphant defeats that rival victories" (Montaigne, French philosopher).

Jeremiah Lanphier: Living for a Greater Cause

What does it mean for workplace believers to live for a cause greater than themselves in our day and time? Jeremiah Lanphier was a businessman in New York City who asked God to do this in his life in 1857.

In a small, darkened room, in the back of one of New York City's lesser churches, a man prayed alone. His request of God was simple, but earth-shattering: "Lord, what wilt Thou have me to do?" [John Woodbridge, ed., *More Than Conquerors* (Chicago, Illinois: Moody Press, 1992), 337]

He was a man approaching midlife without a wife or family, but he had financial means. He made a decision to reject the 'success syndrome" that drove the city's businessmen and bankers. God used this businessman to turn New York City's commercial

I can do everything through Him who gives me strength.

Philippians 4:13

empire on its head. He began a businessmen's prayer meeting on September 23, 1857. The meetings began slowly, but within a few months twenty noonday meetings were convening daily throughout the city. The *New York Tribune* and the *New York Herald* issued articles of revival. It had become the city's biggest news. Now a full-fledged revival, it moved outside New York. By spring of 1858, two thousand met daily in Chicago's Metropolitan Theatre, and in Philadelphia the meetings mushroomed into a four-month-long tent meeting. Meetings were held in Baltimore, Washington, Cincinnati, Chicago, New Orleans, and Mobile. Thousands met to pray because one man stepped out. *Annus Mirabilis*, the year of national revival, had begun.

This was an extraordinary move of God through one man. It was unique because the movement was lead by businessmen, a group long considered the least prone to any form of evangelical fervor, and it had started on Wall Street, the most unlikely of all places to begin. Could God do something extraordinary through you? Take a step. Ask God to do mighty things through you.

Men will rejoice when they see the plumb line in the hand of Zerubbabel.

Zechariah 4:10

Zerubbabel: Becoming a Valued Draft Pick

As children in grammar school we often played pick-up football. Two captains would alternate making the best choices among schoolmates to make up the two teams. I was often chosen first because I was a good athlete. It felt good to be valued by others for what they perceived I could contribute. Conversely, it must have felt crummy to be the last chosen or not chosen at all.

Such was the case for Zerubbabel. He was a man chosen by God to rebuild the temple. God saw something in Zerubbabel that He could use for His purposes. The people also recognized that Zerubbabel was a man in whom they could place their faith. *"So the Lord stirred up the spirit of Zerubbabel son of Shealtiel, governor of Judah, and the spirit of Joshua son of Jehozadak, the high priest, and the spirit of the whole remnant of the people"* (Haggai 1:14).

Are you part of the remnant of workplace believers whom God is calling out today? Do not let the business of today's workplace sidetrack you from the importance of God's agenda for you. Can you recall the day God's Spirit rested on you? Have you walked in that anointing since that day? Satan's strategy is to keep us distracted with the urgency of the moment versus the importance of eternity. Ask God what your priorities should be today. Make His priorities your priorities.

PART 3:
WHAT THE BIBLE SAYS ABOUT WORK

A Selection of Scriptures on Work

God Was a Worker

And on the seventh day God ended His work which He had done, and He rested on the seventh day from all His work which He had done. Then God blessed the seventh day and sanctified it, because in it He rested from all His work which God had created and made. (Gen. 2:2-3 NKJV)

God Worked Six Days a Week

Six days you shall labor and do all your work, but the seventh day is the Sabbath of the Lord your God. (Ex. 20:9 NKJV)

God Would Perform Miracles Through Moses' Work

But take this staff in your hand so you can perform miraculous signs with it. (Ex. 4:17 NIV)

The First Man in the Bible Described As Being Filled with the Spirit of God Was a Craftsman

Then the Lord spoke to Moses, saying: "See, I have called by name Bezalel the son of Uri, the son of Hur, of the tribe of Judah. And I have filled him with the Spirit of God, in wisdom, in understanding, in knowledge, and in all manner of workmanship, to design artistic works, to work in gold, in silver, in bronze, in cutting jewels for setting, in carving wood, and to work in all manner of workmanship. And I, indeed I, have appointed with him Aholiab the son of Ahisamach, of the tribe of Dan; and I have put wisdom in the hearts of all who are gifted artisans, that they may make all that I have commanded you: the tabernacle of meeting, the ark of the Testimony and the mercy seat that is on it, and all the furniture of the tabernacle—the table and its utensils, the pure gold lampstand with all its utensils, the altar of incense, the altar of burnt offering with all its utensils, and the laver and its base—the garments of ministry, the holy garments for Aaron the priest and the garments of his sons, to minister as priests, and the anointing oil and sweet incense for the holy place. According to all that I have commanded you they shall do." (Ex. 31:1-11 NKJV)

God Blessed the Work of Job's Hands
You have blessed the work of his hands, and his possessions have increased in the land. (Job 1:10-11 NKJV)

God Used Workmen to Build the Temple
Moreover there are workmen with you in abundance: woodsmen and stonecutters, and all types of skillful men for every kind of work. Of gold and silver and bronze and iron there is no limit. Arise and begin working, and the Lord be with you.
(1 Chron. 22:15-16 NKJV)

God Gives Us a Desire for the Work We Do
You shall call, and I will answer You;
You shall desire the work of Your hands. (Job 14:15 NKJV)

When We Do Our Work, We Find a Reward in Doing It
For He repays man according to his work,
And makes man to find a reward according to his way.
(Job 34:11 NKJV)

God Reveals God's Work to Us
He seals the hand of every man,
That all men may know His work. (Job 37:7 NKJV)

God's Work Involved the Creation of the Universe

When I consider Your heavens, the work of Your fingers,
The moon and the stars, which You have ordained,
What is man that You are mindful of him,
And the son of man that You visit him? (Ps. 8:3-4 NKJV)

God Establishes Our Work

Let Your work appear to Your servants,
And Your glory to their children.
And let the beauty of the Lord our God be upon us,
And establish the work of our hands for us;
Yes, establish the work of our hands. (Ps. 90:16-17 NKJV)

God Warns Against Slothful Work

He who is slothful in his work
Is a brother to him who is a great destroyer. (Prov. 18:9 NKJV)

God Honors Those Who Do Good Work

Do you see a man who excels in his work?
He will stand before kings;
He will not stand before unknown men. (Prov. 22:29 NKJV)

There Is a Time for Every Work

I said in my heart,
"God shall judge the righteous and the wicked,
For there is a time there for every purpose and for every work."
(Eccl. 3:17 NKJV)

We Are to Find Satisfaction in Our Labor

Nothing is better for a man than that he should eat and drink,
and that his soul should enjoy good in his labor. (Eccl. 2:24 NKJV)

Our Labor Is a Gift of God

I know that nothing is better for them than to rejoice, and to do good in their lives, and also that every man should eat and drink and enjoy the good of all his labor—it is the gift of God. (Eccl. 3:12-13 NKJV)

Here is what I have seen: It is good and fitting for one to eat and drink, and to enjoy the good of all his labor in which he toils under the sun all the days of his life which God gives him; for it is his heritage. As for every man to whom God has given riches and wealth, and given him power to eat of it, to receive his heritage and rejoice in his labor—this is the gift of God. For he will not dwell unduly on the days of his life, because God keeps him busy with the joy of his heart. (Eccl. 5:18-20 NKJV)

Labor Alone Will Not Satisfy the Cry of the Soul

All the labor of man is for his mouth,
And yet the soul is not satisfied. (Eccl. 6:7 NKJV)

Jesus Had a Work to Do

I must work the works of Him who sent Me while it is day; the night is coming when no one can work. As long as I am in the world, I am the light of the world. (John 9:4-6 NKJV)

Jesus Had a Work to Do That Brought Glory to the Father

I have glorified You on the earth. I have finished the work which You have given Me to do. (John 17:4 NKJV)

Jesus Came to Help Us with the Burden of Labor

Come to Me, all you who labor and are heavy laden, and I will give you rest. Take My yoke upon you and learn from Me, for I am gentle and lowly in heart, and you will find rest for your souls. For My yoke is easy and My burden is light. (Matt. 11:28-30 NKJV)

God Calls Us to Examine Our Work

For if anyone thinks himself to be something, when he is nothing, he deceives himself. But let each one examine his own work, and then he will have rejoicing in himself alone, and not in another. For each one shall bear his own load. (Gal. 6:3-5 NKJV)

Our Labor in the Lord Is Not in Vain

Therefore, my beloved brethren, be steadfast, immovable, always abounding in the work of the Lord, knowing that your labor is not in vain in the Lord. (1 Cor. 15:58 NKJV)

Our Labor Is Designed to Allow Us to Help Meet Others' Needs

Let him who stole steal no longer, but rather let him labor, working with his hands what is good, that he may have something to give him who has need. (Eph. 4:28 NKJV)

God Calls Us to Work in Order to Provide for Our Families

For even when we were with you, we commanded you this: If anyone will not work, neither shall he eat. For we hear that there are some who walk among you in a disorderly manner, not working at all, but are busybodies. Now those who are such we command and exhort through our Lord Jesus Christ that they work in quietness and eat their own bread. (2 Thess. 3:10-13 NKJV)

We Were Created to Do Good Works

For we are His workmanship, created in Christ Jesus for good works, which God prepared beforehand that we should walk in them. (Eph. 2:10 NKJV)

There Is a Reward for Doing Our Work Well

And behold, I am coming quickly, and My reward is with Me, to give to every one according to his work. (Rev. 22:12 NKJV)

Our Work Is a Ministry Through Our Gifts and Calling

And He Himself gave some to be apostles, some prophets, some evangelists, and some pastors and teachers, for the equipping of the saints for the work of ministry, for the edifying of the body of Christ, till we all come to the unity of the faith and of the knowledge of the Son of God, to a perfect man, to the measure of the stature of the fullness of Christ; that we should no longer be children, tossed to and fro and carried about with every wind of doctrine, by the trickery of men, in the cunning craftiness of deceitful plotting, but, speaking the truth in love, may grow up in all things into Him who is the head—Christ—from whom the whole body, joined and knit together by what every joint supplies, according to the effective working by which every part does its share, causes growth of the body for the edifying of itself in love. (Eph. 4:11-16 NKJV)

All That We Do Is a Ministry Unto the Lord—Including Our Work

Let every detail in your lives—words, actions, whatever—be done in the name of the Master, Jesus, thanking God the Father every step of the way. (Col. 3:17 THE MESSAGE)

There Is an Inheritance and Reward for Being Faithful to Our Work

And whatever you do, do it heartily, as to the Lord and not to men, knowing that from the Lord you will receive the reward of the inheritance; for you serve the Lord Christ. (Col. 3:23-24 NKJV)

LISTING OF KEY WORKPLACE MINISTRIES

Below are some of the most popular Web sites serving the faith at work movement. Please visit our online directory at **www.icwm.net** for a complete listing of more than twelve hundred organizations. These workplace ministries can be a great resource for your local church.

www.icwm.net
   The International Coalition of Workplace Ministries (ICWM)
www.marketplaceleaders.org
   Marketplace Leaders
www.scruples.net
   Scruples
www.christianity9to5.org
   Christianity 9 to 5
www.faithandworkresources.com
   Faith and Work Resources
www.hischurchatwork.org
   Local Church Ministry Development
www.ivmdl.org/
   Ministry in Daily Life

A complete list of workplace ministries can be found in the *International Faith and Work Directory*, Aslan Group Publishing, 2003. See **www.faithandworkresources.com** to purchase this directory. Also, the entire directory can be accessed online at **www.icwm.net**. Special thanks to Pastor Darryl Bodie of the Fellowship Church in Greensboro for assisting me in compiling this short list for us.

▲ *Avodah Institute*

The primary purpose of The Avodah Institute is to help meet the spiritual needs of people in the marketplace. They accomplish their goal by providing information, ideas, events, and a repository of knowledge and understanding on the issues surrounding the integration of faith and work. http://www.avodahinstitute.com/

▲ *Canadian Tentmakers Network*

Canadian Tentmaker Network (CTN) is a Canada-wide association of individuals and groups committed to tentmaking as a strategy for representing Christ Jesus globally. http://www.tentmakernet.com/

▲ *Christian in Commerce*

Christians in Commerce is an ecumenical Christian organization whose purpose is to bring the presence of Jesus Christ into the marketplace so that it more closely reflects God's will and purpose. We encourage Christian men and women to be Christ in their conduct and example, and to bring truth, integrity and compassion to their workplaces. http://www.christiansincommerce.org/

▲ *Christian Working Woman*

The purpose of The Christian Working Woman is to equip and encourage Christians in the workplace to love Christ more and to demonstrate this love by applying biblical principles to their lives and utilizing their gifts and abilities to build His kingdom. http://www.christianworking-woman.org/

▲ *Executive Ministries*

Executive Ministries exists to equip Christian executives to use the blessing of their business success and community prominence to point their peers to Christ and to disciple them to do the same. The key components of this win-build-send strategy are distinctive evangelistic outreaches and dynamic discipleship Bible studies. Executive Ministries reaches out to business owners, entrepreneurs, corporate officers, senior partners in professional firms, as well as retired executives. http://www.execmin.org/

▲ Faith At Work

Faith at Work (New Zealand) provides training and resources related to career and life planning, the theology of work and vocation, everyday spirituality, ethics for business and the marketplace, and the ministry and mission of the laity in daily life from a Christian perspective. http://www.faithatwork.org.nz/

▲ Faith and Work Resources.com

Faithandworkresources.com is an online ecommerce Website store featuring books, audio and other resources exclusively serving the faith and work movement.
http://wwwfaithandworkresources.com

▲ Faith at Work Magazine

Faith at Work is a national network of progressive Christians at the growing edge of the church: grounded in biblical faith; related to God, self, others and the earth; sustained through intentional community; committed to faith at work in the world. http://www.faithatwork.com/

▲ FaithWorks Magazine

FaithWorks is a bimonthly print and electronic magazine for contemporary Christians. Their mission is to engage Christians in dialogue with their world and empower them to integrate faith and life.
http://www.faithworks.com/

▲ Forum for Faith in the Workplace

The Forum for Faith in the Workplace is an ecumenical Christian association whose mission is to assist individuals in fully applying their personal faith to their work experience, and other aspects of daily living. http://www.faithintheworkplace.org/

▲ Freedom in Christ Ministries

Freedom in Christ is an international, interdenominational ministry that exists to glorify God by prayerfully and strategically equipping and resourcing churches, Christian organizations and mission groups in keeping with the Great Commandment in order to accomplish the Great Commission. http://www.ficm.org/

▲ His Church at Work

HCAW's mission is "Empowering Churches for Workplace Ministry." HCAW seeks to fulfill this mission by assisting local congregations to build sustainable workplace ministries that help their members understand, experience, and carry out their God-given calling of "work as ministry." HCAW offers coaching, tools, and turnkey strategies to launch work life ministry in your church. www.HisChurchatWork.org

▲ International Coalition of Workplace Ministries (ICWM)

The International Coalition of Workplace Ministries (ICWM) is a fellowship of workplace believers who want to ignite leaders for workplace transformation by modeling Jesus Christ. We do this by inspiring, connecting and equipping leaders who want to transform the workplace for Christ. The ICWM website (www.icwm.net) is a clearinghouse for information, resources and organizations in the faith and work movement. http://www.icwm.net

▲ LifeChasers

The mission of LifeChasers is to encourage, inspire and model: (1) How to live out a winsome, genuine faith in a rough-and-tumble world. (2)How to be an effective and strategic influence in culture, believing people are invited by God to be both salt and light. http://www.ficm.org/

▲ Marketplace Christian Network

The purpose of Marketplace Christian Network is a group of Christian worldwide, joined together in one single vision, to actively proclaim the good news of Jesus Christ where we work with words and our lifestyle and be a beacon of light in this decadent age. http://www.marketplacechristian.net/

▲ Marketplace Leaders

Marketplace Leader's purpose is to raise up and train men and women to fulfill their calling in and through the workplace and to view their work as their ministry. Their primary means of accomplishing this is through four key focuses: building unity, training new leaders, publishing and consulting. http://www.marketplaceleaders.org/

▲ *Marketplace Ministries*

Marketplace Ministries is a faith-based employee assistance program and provides a chaplain service to secular businesses. http://www.marketplaceministries.com/

▲ *Marketplace Network*

Marketplace Network is a non-profit organization whose primary mission is to motivate and equip Christians to apply faith to work. They facilitate their mission by providing products and services including: forums, small group curriculum, workshops, classes, resources, study materials and on-line discussion. http://www.marketplace-network.org/

▲ *Mennonite Economic Development Associates (MEDA)*

Mennonite Economic Development Associates is an association of persons who are committed to the nurture and expression of their Christian faith in a business or work setting. http://www.meda.org/

▲ *Mockler Center*

The Colman M. Mockler Center equips the church and its members to bring the work of Christ into the activities of daily life, especially life in the workplace. The Center engages in education, direct ministry, and research to bring the resources of Biblical interpretation, Christian theology and ethics, and practical ministry into the working world. Its mission is carried out in three areas: in the Gordon-Conwell community, in partnership with churches, and directly in the workplace. http://www.gordonconwell.edu/ockenga/mockler/

▲ *Needle's Eye Ministries, Inc.*

NEM, an interdenominational ministry, seeks to present Jesus Christ to persons in the workplace, to encourage the development of their Christian lifestyle and leadership, and to support the local church in marketplace issues. http://www.needleseye.org/

▲ *Priority Associates*

Priority Associates is a resource to business and professional men and women, helping them to develop spiritually, personally, and professionally. http://www.priorityassociates.org/

▲ *Scruples*

The Scruples web site is a resource for marketplace Christians. Contents includes: a calendar, directory, forums, library, links publications and seminars. http://www.scruples.net/

▲ *The Crossroads Center for Faith and Work*

The Crossroads Center for Faith and Work serves women and men of all faiths, by surfacing the connections and blurring the lines between faith, spirituality, and deepest values and day-to-day work as professionals, volunteers, homemakers and family members. http://www.crossroads-center.org/

▲ *The Faith & Work Project*

This site researches and promotes the application of Christian faith and values to business and organizational life. http://users.aol.com/faith-work/

▲ *The High Calling of Our Daily Work*

TheHighCalling.org aims to connect people in the ordinary circumstances of life with the faith that undergirds and sustains all that we do. Howard E. Butt, Jr., has dedicated his life to both a family business and a ministry for Christian lay renewal. His vision for the vital role of the laity in the church and daily life has led him to write several books and produce one-minute radio spots entitled The High Calling of Our Daily Work. This site is an effort to provide you with a tool to delve deeper into the concepts introduced in those spots. https://www.thehighcalling.org/

▲ *Value of the Person*

Through consulting, seminars, books and other products, Value of the Person, promotes Theory "R" Management. More than just a program, Value of the Person connects the head and heart, the workplace and the home. http://www.valueoftheperson.com/

▲ *WOWI - Workplace Wisdom Interactive*

WOWI is a global Christian alliance dedicated to teaching individuals how to integrate and effectively apply Biblical principles in the workplace by helping them to strengthen their relationship with God. Their mission is to encourage individual believers to make a positive difference in their workplace and community and to encourage unity in the body of Christ. http://www.wowi.net/

▲ *WorkLife Resource Center*

The WorkLife Resource Center is a global resource center for the working Christian. This site is an "Amazon.com" type site for the workplace movement, bringing a large selection of discounted resources together in one place for distribution to churches and those in the workplace. www.WorkplaceMinistry.com

PUBLICATIONS/NEWSLETTERS

▲ *Business Reform magazine*

Business Reform exists to assist Christian businesses and businesspeople in giving glory to God by applying the Word of the Lord to our work on earth.
http://businessreform.com/BusinessReform.php

▲ *Christian Working Woman* e-mail newsletter is directed at women in the workplace. http://www.christianworkingwoman.org/

▲ *My WorkLife Toolbox*

Workplace Toolbox is a free weekly discipleship resource sponsored by His Church at Work containing writings and helps from various leaders and writers in the workplace movement.
http://www.WorkLifeToolbox.org

▲ *Regent Business Review*

Regent Business Review is an electronic magazine published by the Regent University Graduate School of Business. The mission of RBR is

to equip and encourage Christians to be more God-honoring leaders and managers.
http://www.regent.edu/acad/schbus/maz/busreview/home.htm

▲ *Marketplace Moments*

E-mail devotional Christ-centered teaching on issues of concern to men and women in the workplace. This online devotion now reaches subscribers in over 40 states and 10 foreign countries. http://www.market-place-network.org

▲ *TGIF Today God Is First*

TGIF Today God Is First daily devotional e-mail written by Os Hillman is available free via email. Take a scripture verse and applies a workplace situation. Thousands subscribe from around the world to this helpful tool. http://www.marketplaceleaders.org

PROFESSIONS/ MEMBERSHIP-BASED GROUP

▲ *Affiliation of Christian Engineers (ACE)*

ACE is a newly-formed "virtual" organization of and for Christian engineers, around the world. In keeping with their technical professional focus, ACE is committed to using the best of today's technology to bring value to its members. Stated simply, they believe that ACE should add value—to its members, to the engineering profession, to society at large, and to the Body of Christ. The purpose of ACE is to provide its members numerous ways to network and obtain information relevant to the profession of engineering and their common faith. Thereby, ACE will encourage its members to be "salt, light, and leaven" in their places of employment and in the engineering profession as a whole.
http://christianengineer.net/

▲ *Business & Professional Ministry*

Sponsored by the Navigators, this site exists to help business and professionals integrate and extend their faith. http://www.bpnavigators.org/

▲ Business & Professional Network

The mission of the BPN is to facilitate business investment by Christians of the 1st World with believers in poor and developing countries that will enhance the welfare of those nations and contribute to the work of the Gospel. http://www.bpn.org/

▲ Businessmen's Fellowship USA

To change to culture of the marketplace by impacting men for Christ, empowering them with His Holy Spirit, and dedicating their lives and resources to change the world. http://www.bmfusa.com

▲ Christian International Business Network

To equip Christian business people to operate in the supernatural power of God and to practice biblical principles in the marketplace. http://www.ciministries.org

▲ Christian Leadership Ministries

The mission of Christian Leadership Ministries is to reach and equip professors to change the world for Christ. http://www.clm.org/

▲ CBMC

CBMC is Connecting Business Men to Christ, a worldwide network of business and professional men. Established in 1930 by a small group of businessmen, who shared the desire to communicate the eternal, life-saving message of Jesus Christ to others, CBMC continues to evangelize and disciple today's business and professional community. http://www.cbmc.com/

▲ CBMC International

CBMC International is a network of business and professional people in over 80 nations. You would find CBMC members in virtually every business and profession, both men and women, but all are committed to the basic premise that they have been "called" to be in ministry in the marketplace. http://www.cbmcint.org/

▲ Christian Medical & Dental Society

The Christian Medical & Dental Associations mission is to motivate, educate, and equip Christian physicians and dentists to glorify God. http://www.cmds.org/

▲ Corporate Chaplains of America

Corporate Chaplains of America (CCA) provides genuine "Caring in the Workplace" through its workforce of "Certified Workplace Chaplains." The mission of CCA is to build relationships with employees through chaplains with the hope of gaining permission to share the good news of Jesus Christ in a non-threatening manner. http://www.iamchap.org/

▲ Fellowship of Companies for Christ International

FCCI, the Fellowship of Companies for Christ International, is an organization—a fellowship—that exists to minister not just "to" you, but "through" you to the companies you represent. http://www.christianity.com/fcci

▲ Full Gospel Businessmen's Fellowship International

The Full Gospel Business Men's Fellowship International is an organization founded to reach men in all nations for Jesus Christ and to call men back to God. http://www.fgbmfi.org

▲ International Christian Chamber of Commerce

To serve as a vehicle in extending the operation and principles of wisdom, love and rule of God into the marketplaces of the world. Chapters in more than 80 countries. http://www.iccc.net

▲ International Fellowship of Christians Businessmen

To establish and develop a worldwide Christian business and professional men's organization with men of destiny who desire to be pacesetters and world changers, excelling in all aspects of life and business. http://www.ifcb.org

▲ InterVarsity MBA Ministry

This ministry ministers to MBA students attending business schools throughout the United States. http://www.intervarsity.org/grad/mba/

▲ Media Fellowship International

The mission of Media FellowshipInternational (MFI) is reaching media and entertainment professionals worldwide for Christ. The vision of MFI is to minister among media and entertainment professionals in key arts and media cities worldwide who are seeking safe spiritual haven; transforming them into Christian leaders who serve, challenge, and influence. http://www.mediafellowship.org

▲ Nurses Christian Fellowship

In response to God's love, grace and truth: The Purpose of Nurses Christian Fellowship, as a ministry of InterVarsity Christian Fellowship/USA is to establish and advance in nursing, within education and practice, witnessing communities of nursing students and nurses who follow Jesus as Savior and Lord: growing in love—for God, God's Word,God's people of every ethnicity and culture and God's purposes in the world. http://www.intervarsity.org/ncf/

▲ The Godly Business Woman

The goal of this site is to educate, inspire and encourage women to be all they can be through Jesus Christ. They want to be a resource on which women can depend and shed light on God's view of the responsibilities women have been given.
http://www.godlybusinesswoman.com/

▲ With You Always

These drawings depict ordinary people in their everyday environment, with the addition of showing the presence of Jesus Christ and His involvement in those routine activities. The objective of this "With you always" series is to help Christians everywhere visualize the reality of Jesus' presence in their lives at all times, particularly during those everyday tasks where we spend most of our time.
http://members.aol.com/JesusImages/index.htm

▲ Young Business Leaders

Professional outreach from Briarwood Presbyterian Church in Birmingham, AL. http://www.ybl.org/

CAREERS

▲ *Intercristo*

Intercristo is a Christian job-referral service. They match Christians with jobs in Christian non-profit organizations, based upon their expertise, education, geographic preference, and compensation concerns. http://www.jobleads.org/

CHURCHES/DENOMINATIONS

▲ *CenteredLife–CenteredWork*

The mission of this Lutheran organization is to awaken and align personal and organizational callings to live faithfully in God's world and to equip Christians to live out their faith within God's world. http://www.luthersem.edu/clcw/

▲ *His Church at Work*

The mission of His Church at Work is to encourage the Church to join God where He is moving in the workplace, assisting pastors and the local church in helping men and woman understand, experience, and fulfill their God-given calling of work as ministry. http://hischurchatwork.org/

LEADERSHIP

▲ *De Pree Leadership Center*

The De Pree Leadership Center cultivates the character of leaders and encourages the integration of faith and public life. They facilitate conversations, mentoring relationships, and alliances across occupational lines in order to forge more collaborative forms of leadership. The Center's primary concerns are with personal and institutional transformation grounded in spiritual as well as moral commitments. http://www.depree.org/

▲ *The Robert K. Greenleaf Center for Servant-Leadership*

The goal of The Greenleaf Center is to help people understand the principles and practices of servant-leadership; to nurture colleagues and institutions by providing a focal point and opportunities to share thoughts and ideas on servant-leadership; to produce and publish new resources by others on servant-leadership; and to connect servant-leaders in a network of learning. http://www.greenleaf.org/

"OTHER"

▲ *Koinonia Partners*
Koinonia Partners, Inc. is a Christian organization seeking to be a "demonstration plot for the Kingdom of God". They are committed to non-violence and peaceful solutions to society's problems, reconciliation among all people, Christian discipleship, and the empowerment of the poor, the neglected and the oppressed.
http://www.koinoniapartners.org/

▲ *The Alban Institute*
The mission of the Alban Institute is to gather, generate, and provide practical knowledge across denominational lines thorough action research, books and periodicals, consulting and training services, and education seminars for those involved with congregations.
http://www.alban.org/

Endnotes

INTRODUCTION
1. Doug Spada, *HisChurchatWork.org*

Section One: Background of the Workplace Ministry Movement

CHAPTER 1
1. Os Hillman, *Regent Business Review* article, November 2003,
   The Faith and Work Movement: Opening the 9 to 5 Window.

CHAPTER 2
1. Os Guinness, *The Call* (Nashville: Word Publishing, 1998), p.32.
2. Rich Marshall, *God@Work,* (Destiny Image Publishers, 2000), p. 5.
3. John Beckett, *Loving Monday* (Colorado Springs: NavPress), p. 69.
4. *BreakPoint*, Sept. 1, 2003.
5. Doug Sherman and William Hendricks, *Your Work Matters to God*
   (Colorado Springs: NavPress, 1987), p. 60.
6. *Word in Life Study Bible* (Nashville: Thomas Nelson Publishers,
   1993), p. 1869 notes.
7. Os Hillman, *Faith & Work: Do They Mix?* (Cumming, GA: Aslan
   Group Publishing, 2000), p. 11.

CHAPTER 3
1. Doug Sherman radio interview, Discovery House Publishers,
   published in 2000 in audio cassette.
2. *Sales & Marketing Magazine*, Feb. 2001.
3. Princeton Religion Research Center.
4. Doug Sherman, author, *Your Work Matters to God*, Interview,
   Discover the Word Radio Bible Class, Discovery House Publishers,
   published in 2000 in audio cassette.
5. Mark Greene, *Supporting Christians at Work* (Birmingham, UK:
   Administry), p. 5.
6. 1998 U.S. Bureau of Labor Statistics.

Section Two: Workplace Ministry in the Local Church

CHAPTER 4

1. Gunnar Olson, Plastic Bag Story, *TGIF Today God Is First*, by Os Hillman, (Destiny Image Publishers, 2000), p. 121.

CHAPTER 5

1. Mark Greene, *Supporting Christians at Work* (Birmingham, UK: Administry), p. 5.
2. George Barna and Mark Hatch, *Boiling Point* (Ventura, CA: Regal Books, 2001), chapter: "The Future of the Local Church."
3. Life Works Seminar, New Haven, CT, February 2003.
4. *Anointed for Business* (Ventura, CA: Regal Publishing, 2002), inside cover endorsement.
5. Doug Spada, *His Church at Work.*

CHAPTER 6

1. An interview and dialogue with Dr. Henry Blackaby, moderated by John Beckett, chairman, Intercessors for America, September 18, 2001.

Section Three: Implementation of Workplace Ministry in the Local Church

CHAPTER 7

1. Doug Spada and David Scott, excerpted from *Regent Business Review*, November 2003, reprinted with permission (Regent University, 2004).

CHAPTER 8

1. *TGIF Today God Is First*, by Os Hillman, (Destiny Image Publishers, 2000), December 7 devotion.
2. Kent Humphreys, *Lasting Investments* (Colorado Springs: NavPress, 2004), chapter 1. To order from their web site: www.navpress.org.

CHAPTER 9

1. Wooddale Church is a His Church at Work partner church. These results have been obtained from this church's obedience to God's

call in this area and an intentional focused process. *www.HisChurchatWork.org.*

2. Journey Community Church is a His Church at Work partner church. These results have been obtained from this church's obedience to God's call in this area and an intentional focused process. *www.HisChurchatWork.org.*

CHAPTER 10

1. Pete Hammond directs the Ministry in Daily Life for InterVarsity Christian Fellowship. *www.ivmdl.org.*

CHAPTER 12

1. Mark Greene, *Supporting Christians at Work* (Birmingham, UK: Administry), p. 6.

2. Anne Rowthorn, *The Liberation of the Laity*, (Wilton, CT: Morehouse-Barlow, 1986), p. 25.

3. Elton Trueblood, *The Incendiary Fellowship* (NY: Harper & Row, 1967), p. 126.

4. Gary Rowlandson quoted in "Supporting Christians at Work," Mark Greene, London Institute of Contemporary Christianity, p. 126.

5. Eric Swanson is a Leadership Community Director for Leadership Network and serves as a consultant with CitiReach Int'l. Eric is also coauthor of *The Externally Focused Church*, Group Publishers, June 2004.

SUMMARY

1. Malcolm Gladwell, *Tipping Point*, (Back Bay Books, 2003), p.19.

2. Ibid., p. 34.

3. www.valuebasedmanagement.net/methods_rogers_innovation_adoption_curve.html.

4. International Faith and Work Directory, www.icwm.net, International Coalition of Workplace Ministries.

APPENDIX 2

1. Mark Greene, *Supporting Christians at Work* (Birmingham, UK: Administry), p. 27.

BIBLIOGRAPHY

Dr. Peter Wagner has graciously allowed me to reprint the following bibliography of workplace books that he has personally reviewed and provided a one sentence assessment. This is not a complete list on the subject. For a complete list see Pete Hammond's *The Marketplace Annotated Bibliography: A Christian Guide to Books on Work*, Business & Vocation, IVP, 2002. To purchase many of these resources visit www.faithandworkresources.com.

Workplace Ministries Reading & Resource List

Compiled by C. Peter Wagner *(Last revised 1-1-04)*

Introduction. The most complete bibliography on workplace ministries, listed below under Pete Hammond, et. al., contains comments on no less than twelve hundred related works. The books I have listed here are only those in my personal library, and all of which I have read. This turns out to be a much larger area of discussion than most Christian leaders are aware of, and I believe it will soon be one of the hottest subjects in the body of Christ. An interesting indicator of this is that of the sixty-six books on this list in October 2002, no fewer than thirty-one, or 47 percent, were written since 2000.

A potential area of conflict is the rather striking gap in understanding the different cultures of what I like to call the "nuclear church" leadership as over against the "extended church" (workplace) leadership. My sense is that it will take until 2010 to come to terms with the God-designed synergism between the two forms of the church.

One theme running through these books, especially the earlier ones, is how to be a good Christian out there in the workplace or in the "world." A later emphasis comes in defining a Christian's role in the workplace as "ministry" *per se*. Some newer books attempt to describe the gap between the nuclear church and the extended church and analyze how godly behavior might differ between the two.

Banks, Robert and Kimberly Powell, Editors. *Faith in Leadership: How Leaders Live out Their Faith in Their Work and Why it Matters.* San Francisco, CA: Jossey-Bass Inc., Publishers, 2000, 214 pp. A scholarly-oriented look by fourteen authors at the challenges of expressing faith in the workplace.

Beckett, John D., *Loving Monday: Succeeding in Business without Selling Your Soul.* Downers Grove, IL: InterVarsity Press, 1998, 176 pp. An insightful story about how John Beckett operates in the marketplace with many references to other people and books as well.

Beehner, John F., *True Wealth By the Book: How 100 Inspirational Americans Learned Character, Moral, and Spiritual Truths.* Jacksonville, FL: By The Book Publishing, 1999, 262 pp. Not just testimonies, but insightful analyses of each one with practical applications. (DEVOTIONAL)

Briner, Bob. *The Management Methods of Jesus.* Nashville, TN: Thomas Nelson, 1996, 111 pp. About 50 two-page devotional-type thoughts applying the teaching of Jesus to business and daily life.

Briner, Bob. *Roaring Lambs: A Gentle Plan to Radically Change Your World.* Grand Rapids, MI: Zondervan, 1993, 179 pp. A challenge for Christians in the marketplace to move proactively to change society.

Brook, Linda Rios, *Wake Me When It's Over: From the Boardroom to the Twilight Zone and the Faithfulness of God.* Baltimore, MD: AmErica House, 2002, 191 pp. A fast-moving story of how a television executive's Christian principles put her between a rock and a hard place, and how God brought her out a winner. Brook is a member of the International Coalition of Apostles.

Buford, Bob. *Half Time: Changing Your Game Plan from Success to Significance.* Grand Rapids, MI: Zondervan Publishing House, 1994, 192 pp. A businessman who grew a successful cable television company at mid-age founded Leadership Network. (www.leadnet.org). www.halftime.org.

Stuck in Half Time: Reinvesting Your One and Only Life. Grand Rapids, MI: Zondervan Publishing House, 2001, 145 pp. A practical, motivational look at how to steer toward your greatest life potential, especially if you have made enough to retire in your forties.

Game Plan: Winning Strategies for the Second Half of Your Life. Grand Rapids, MI: Zondervan Publishing House, 1997, 163 pp. Strategizing the way to move your life forward as you advance in life.

Burkett, Larry. *Business by the Book: The Complete Guide of Biblical Principles for the Workplace.* Nashville, TN: Thomas Nelson Publishers, 1998, 292 pp. The author provides business principles from his own experience as well as from God's word.

The Businesswoman's Topical Bible. Tulsa, OK, Honor Books, no date (after 1984), 320 pp. 98 topics related to the workplace with relevant Bible verses (NIV) under each one. (DEVOTIONAL)

Copeland, Germaine. *Prayers that Avail Much for the Workplace.* Tulsa, OK: Harrison House, 2001, 292 pp. 87 topics related to life in the workplace with a written prayer under each one. The "Executive Edition" is printed on Bible paper and bound in leather. (DEVOTIONAL).

Crane, Christopher A. and Mike Hamel. *Executive Influence: Impacting Your Workplace for Christ.* Colorado Springs, CO: NavPress, 2003, 185 pp. Case studies showing how forty executives and professionals relate their faith to their work.

Daniels, Peter J. *How to Be Happy Though Rich.* Unley Park, South Australia: The House of Tabor, 1984, 125 pp. An upbeat discussion on various aspects of wealth from a Christian point of view.

Deal, John. *Decisions by the Book.* Richmond, VA: Insight to Freedom, Inc., 1991, 1995 310 pp. This book provides a biblical guide for making accurate decisions in the home, government business and employment. Fully indexed. (DEVOTIONAL)

DeMoss, Ted and Robert Tamasy. *The Gospel and the Briefcase: The Art of Presenting Christ to Business and Professional People.* Chattanooga, TN: Christian Business Men's Committee of USA, 1984, 146 pp. How Ted DeMoss learned to share his faith in the marketplace.

Diehl, William. *The Monday Connection.* HarperCollins, 1993, 200 pp. The author focuses on how to connect the faith of Sunday with the operational faith of Monday. This book is mainline-oriented and very well thought out.

Flowers, Lois. *Women, Faith, and Work: How Ten Successful Business Professionals Blend Belief and Business.* Nashville, TN: Word Publishing, 2001, 165 pp. A top book on how women fit into marketplace ministry written in a biographical format.

Gazelka, Paul. *Marketplace Ministers: Awakening God's People in the Workplace to Their Ultimate Purpose.* Lake Mary, FL: Creation House Press, 2003, 148 pp. Paul Gazelka is a prime example of a marketplace person coming to recognize their ministry in the marketplace. Furthermore, he analyzes it well and draws important principles for all of us.

Graves, Stephen R., and Thomas G. Addington. *The Fourth Frontier: Exploring the New World of Work.* Nashville, TN: Word Publishing, 2000, 200 pp. How to rely on biblical principles to guide you in marketplace ministry.

Daily Focus: Daily Readings for Integrating Faith in the Workplace. Nashville, TN: W Publishing Group, 2001, 334 pp. A scripture and a devotional thought for each day of the year. (DEVOTIONAL)

Green, Mark. *Thank God It's Monday: Ministry in the Workplace.* Bletchley, England: Scripture Union, 1994, 2001, 180 pp. Good insights on why a believer's work should be considered a ministry.

Hammond, Pete, R. Paul Stevens, and Todd Svanoe. *The Marketplace Annotated Bibliography: A Christian Guide to Books on Work, Business & Vocation.* Downers Grove, IL: Inter-Varsity Press, 2002, 220 pp. An informative list of 1200 marketplace-faith books with more than a dozen thematic indexes.

Hamon, Bill. *The Day of the Saints: Equipping Believers for their Revolutionary Role in Ministry.* Shippensburg, PA: Destiny Image, 2002, 430 pp. Although the book is much broader, 86 pages of it (Chapters 7 & 8) contain some of the finest material on marketplace ministries to date. Hamon is a member of the International Coalition of Apostles.

Hamon, Bill, Sharon Stone, and Richard Fleming. *Hearing the Voice of God in the Marketplace.* Brookmans Park, England: Christian International Europe Business Network, 2002, 103 pp. A workbook designed to activate prophecy among workplace ministers.

Hamon, Jane. *The Cyrus Decree: Releasing apostolic and prophetic keys to the twenty-first century Church to liberate captives, transfer wealth, revolutionize nations and build the Kingdom of God.* Santa Rosa Beach, FL: published by the author, 2001, 211 pp. The sub-title says it all. Excellent biblical insights.

Hester, Marcus. *The God Factor: Getting the Edge at Work.* Shippensburg, PA: Destiny Image, 2003. An excellent perspective on workplace ministry by one who has been deeply involved in both cultures. Hester is a member of the International Coalition of Apostles.

High, David R. *Kings & Priests.* Oklahoma City, OK: Books for Children of the World, 1993. A small book arguing that priest (pastors) must be linked to kings (workplace believers) in order for God's plans to be accomplished.

Hill, Alexander. *Just Business.* Downers Grove, IL: InterVarsity Press, 1997, 232 pp. This is an excellent textbook on how to apply Christian ethics in the marketplace.

Hillman, Os. *The Purposes of Money: Exposing the Five Fallacies About Money and God's Five Purposes for its Use.* Cumming, GA: Aslan Group Publishing, 2000, 67 pp. Os Hillman is one of the most respected leaders, as well as one of the most prolific authors, in the field of marketplace ministries. Here he presents a biblical view of wealth. Hillman is a member of the International Coalition of Apostles.

Proven Strategies for Business Success. Cumming, GA: Aslan Group Publishing, 1993, 65 pp. A practical primer on marketing.

Today God Is First: 365 Meditations on the Principles of Christ in the Workplace. Shippensburg, PA: Destiny Image Publishers, 2000, 384 pp. A daily devotional for the businessperson. Also available free on the Internet at InJesus.com/subscriptions. (DEVOTIONAL) Hardback.

Today God Is First 4-Minute Meditations. Shippensburg, PA: Destiny Image Publishers, 2000, 285 pp. Similar to the above, but organized by topics. (DEVOTIONAL) Paperback.

Today God Is First Small Group Bible Study. Cumming, GA: Aslan Group Publishing, 2002, 46 pp. Twelve marketplace-related studies that can be used either by individuals or in small groups.

Adversity & Pain: The Gifts That Nobody Wants. Cumming, GA: Aslan Group Publishing, 1996, 93 pp. Godly approaches toward handling the inevitable crises that the marketplace produces.

Faith & Work: Do They Mix? Discovering God's Purposes for Your Work. Cumming, GA: Aslan Group Publishing, 2000, 108 pp. Understanding that your work is your ministry. This is one of the top books on the list.

Making Godly Decisions: How to Know and do the Will of God. Cumming, GA: Aslan Group Publishing, 2000, 74 pp. Biblical ways for making the right decisions at the right time.

Are You A Biblical Worker? Cumming, GA, Aslan Group Publishing, 2003, 36 page workbook, self-assessment test designed for Bible study use.

Hodge, Ian. *Making Sense of Your Dollars: A Biblical Approach to Wealth.* Vallecito, CA: Ross House Books, 1995, 177 pp. The creation and use of wealth in a biblical context.

Humphreys, Kent & Davidene. *Show and then Tell: Presenting the Gospel through Daily Encounters.* Chicago, IL: Moody Press, 2000 194 pp. How to fulfill our Christian responsibilities in the marketplace, especially the ministry of evangelism. Kent is a member of the International Coalition of Apostles.

Hybels, Bill. *Christians in the Marketplace: Making Your Faith Work on the Job.* Wheaton, IL: Victor Books, 1982, 144 pp. Practical thoughts about work from a successful pastor.

Jones, Laurie Beth. *Jesus CEO: Using Ancient Wisdom for Visionary Leadership.* New York, NY: Hyperion, 1995, 305 pp. A successful businesswoman, the author draws leadership principles from the life of Jesus. (DEVOTIONAL).

The Path: Creating Your Mission Statement for Work and for Life. New York, NY: Hyperion, 1996, 231 pp. A practical, faith-oriented textbook on defining and fulfilling the mission of your business or profession. Not much about ministry here.

Julian, Larry. *God is my CEO: Following God's Principles in a Bottom-Line World.* Holbrook, MA: Adams Media Corporation, 2001, 241 pp. Personal vignettes of 20 believers who have made it in the marketplace. Not much explicit reference to ministry.

Klingaman, Patrick. *Thank God It's Monday: Making Business Your Ministry.* Wheaton, IL: Victor Books, 1996, 196 pp. A businessman discovers how work is a ministry and carefully analyzes the perspectives behind this truth. Chapters 1-5 are very relevant to the relationship between the nuclear church and the extended church.

Kriegbaum, Richard. *Leadership Prayers.* Wheaton, IL: Tyndale House Publishers, 1998, 120 pp. Thirty prayers on topics relevant to the every day life of business people. (DEVOTIONAL).

Life@Work Co., *The Life@Work Book: Sixteen Respected Leaders Talk about Blending Biblical Wisdom and Business Excellence.* Nashville, TN: Word Publishing, 2000, 163 pp. Top names from John Maxwell to Bill Hybels to Max DePree, etc., address the subject

Mackenzie, Alistair and Wayne Kirkland. *Where's God on Monday?* Christchurch, NZ: NavPress NZ. 2002, 108 pp. A solid book on the basics of workplace ministry.

Marr, Steve. *Business Proverbs: Daily Wisdom for the Marketplace.* Grand Rapids, MI: Fleming H. Revell, 2001, 254 pp. A scripture, a devotional thought and a Proverb for every day of the year with a topical index. (DEVOTIONAL)

Marshall, Rich. *God @ Work: Discovering the Anointing for Business.* Shippensburg, PA: Destiny Image Publishers, Inc., 2000, 142 pp. The major principle in this book is that your business is your ministry. Marshall is a member of the International Coalition of Apostles.

Murdock, Mike. *The 1 Minute Businessman's Devotional* and *The 1 Minute Businesswoman's Devotional.* Denton, TX: Wisdom International, 1992, 204 pp. Pithy 2-page Bible-oriented thoughts. Separate covers for each gender.

Nash, Laura. *Believers in Business: Resolving the Tensions Between Christian Faith, Business Ethics, Competition, and Our Definitions of Success.* Nashville, TN: Thomas Nelson, 1994, 295 pp. A survey of evangelical CEOs and their attitudes toward relating the workplace to their faith. Many consider this a classic in the field.

Nash, Laura and Scotty McLennan. *Church on Sunday, Work on Monday: The Challenge of Fusing Christian Values with Business Life.* San Francisco, CA: Jossey-Bass, 2001, 283 pp. An extremely valuable sociological study of the differences between the church and the marketplace based on extensive interviews.

Novak, Michael. *Business as a Calling: Work and the Examined Life.* New York, NY: The Free Press, 1996, 205 pp. An intellectually stimulating philosophy of business as a virtuous vocation or calling.

Nix, William. *Transforming Your Workplace for Christ.* Broadman & Holman Publishers, 1997, 210 pp. Includes ten Christian values every workplace needs.

Oliver, David. *Work: Prison or Place of Destiny?* Word Publishing, 2001, 218 pp. An English business leader teaches that work in the marketplace is actually ministry.

Oliver, David and James Thwaites. *Church that Works.* Milton Keynes, England: Word Publishing, 2001, 220 pp. Strong on Hebrew vs. Greek thinking and that the church exists both within and without the gathered church.

Olson, Gunnar. *Business Unlimited.* Orebro, Sweden: International Christian Chamber of Commerce, 2002, 223 pp. An autobiography of the founder of the International Christian Chamber of Commerce.

One-Minute Pocket Bible for the Business Professional. Tulsa, OK: Honor Books, no date, 126 pp. 111 topics related to business with Bible verses (NKJV) under each one. (DEVOTIONAL)

Oster, Merrill and Mike Hamel. *The Entrepreneur's Creed: The Principles and Passions of 20 Successful Entrepreneurs.* Nashville, TN: Broadman & Holman Publishers, 2001, 215 pp. Stories of 20 Christian entrepreneurs who have developed principles in the marketplace rooted in their faith. A total of 161 principles appear in this book.

Peabody, Larry. *Secular Work Is Full-Time Service.* Fort Washington, PA: Christian Literature Crusade, 1974, 142 pp. A well thought out apologetic for marketplace ministry. I would rank this 30-year old book as the top theology of marketplace ministry.

Peacocke, Dennis. *Doing Business God's Way!* Santa Rosa, CA: Rebuild, 1995 revised edition 2003, 163 pp. Eleven master principles upon which business should be built. Peacocke is a member of the International Coalition of Apostles.

The Emperor Has No Clothes: Commentaries. Santa Rosa, CA: Strategic Christian Services, 2002, 179 pp. Two to four-page thoughts on vital aspects of life in the marketplace. These 56 "commentaries" could profitably be read as a devotional, although the book is not set up in that way. (DEVOTIONAL)

Pierce, Chuck D. and Rebecca Wagner Sytsema, *The Future War of the Church.* Ventura, CA: Renew, 2001, 292 pp. The whole book is good, but the chapter most relevant to marketplace is Chapter 6, "The Transference of Wealth." Pierce is a member of the International Coalition of Apostles.

Pierce, Gregory F.A. *Spirituality @ Work: 10 Ways to Balance Your Life on the Job.* Chicago, IL: Loyola Press, 2001, 161 pp. How to bring spirituality into the marketplace in order to find fulfillment in your work.

Pollard, C. William. *The Soul of the Firm.* Grand Rapids, MI: Zondervan Publishing House, 1996, 163 pp. How Pollard applies business and Christian principles to the success of ServiceMaster.

Powell, Edward A. and Rousas John Rushdoony. *Tithing and Dominion.* Vallecito, CA: Ross House Books, 1979, 143 pp. A very thorough philosophical/theological argument for the necessity of tithing to fulfill God's purpose for your life and your business.

Rogers, Mike and Debi Rogers. *The Kingdom Agenda: Experiencing God in Your Workplace.* Nashville, TN: LifeWay Press, 1997, 94 pp. A practical six-week Bible study guide to show how the marketplace can become your mission field. kingdommr@aol.com. (DEVOTIONAL)

Ruddick, Morris E. *The Joseph-Daniel Calling: Facilitating the Release of the Wealth of the Wicked.* An excellent understanding of the potential of the transference of huge amounts of wealth to the kingdom of God, and how we need to be prepared for it.

Rush, Myron. *Management: A Biblical Approach.* Colorado Springs, CO: Victor, 2002, 228 pp. Sound principles of leadership molded by Christian principles.

Rushdoony, R.J. and Otto J. Scott, Editors. *Journal of Christian Reconstruction. Vol. X, No. 2.* Vallecito, CA: Chalcedon, 1984, 262 pp. A somewhat dated and scholarly compilation of essays by leading theologians, businessmen, and pastors dealing with Christianity, business and economics. This takes the position that God's people are obligated to change society according to God's values.

Serra, Jack. *Marketplace Marriage & Revival: The Spiritual Connection.* Orlando, FL: Longwood Communications, 2001, 141 pp. Jack Serra argues that the influence that a marketplace minister will have depends heavily on how that person's marriage is handled. The book is also seasoned with gems of general advice from a successful businessperson.

Sherman, Doug and William Hendricks. *Your Work Matters to God.* Colorado Springs, CO: Navpress, 1987, 286 pp. A thoughtful theology of work, written in the earlier days of the faith and work movement.

Silbiger, Steven. *The Jewish Phenomenon: Seven Keys to the Enduring Wealth of a People.* Atlanta, GA: Longstreet Press, 2000, 250 pp. This is not a book directly on ministry in the workplace, but it is excellent in showing how the Hebrew mindset relates to creation of wealth.

Silvoso, Ed. *Anointed for Business: How Christians Can Use Their Influence in the Marketplace to Change the World.* Ventura, CA: Regal Books, 2002, 195 pp. This book sets the standard for understanding the teaching of the Bible and its application to marketplace ministry today. Silvoso is a member of the International Coalition of Apostles.

God's Ticker Tape: A Report on Divine Acquisitions in the Marketplace. San Jose, CA: Harvest Evangelism, 2003, 78 pp. Forty-six brief testimonies of how the workplace provides opportunity for ministry.

Tamasy, Robert J., Editor. *Jesus Works Here: Leading Christians in Business Talk About How You Can Walk With Christ Through Stress, Change, and Other Challenges of the Workplace.* Nashville, TN: Broadman & Holman Publishers, 1995, 255 pp. Insights on dimensions of the workplace from the Christian perspective from 47 members of the Christian Business Men's Committee (CBMC).

The Complete Christian Businessman. Brentwood, TN: Wolgemuth & Hyatt, Publishers, 1991, 377 pp. In this volume 75 authors address issues of marketplace ministry.

Thompson, Robb. *Excellence in the Workplace.* Tinley Park, IL: Family Harvest Church, 2002, 298 pp. An upbeat, motivational book to help you leave mediocrity and move to a higher level in the workplace.

Thwaites, James. *The Church Beyond the Congregation: The strategic role of the church in the postmodern era.* Carlisle, England, Paternoster Press, 1999, 291 pp. A very insightful work dealing with the philosophy underlying the faith and work movement. He clearly explains the difference between Greek and Hebrew thinking.

Renegotiating the Church Contract: The death and life of the 21st Century church. Carlisle, England: Paternoster Press, 2001, 230 pp. Great philosophical detail on how platonic (Greek) thought is killing the church as we know it.

Tsukahira, Peter. *My Father's Business: Guidelines for Ministry in the Marketplace.* Israel, Self-published, 2000, 174 pp. A stimulating presentation of bringing faith to the workplace and seeing your occupation as a divine calling. Recognition that the church and marketplace have two different cultures.

Watts, Julian. *God's Business: Preparing the Church for Dramatic Growth.* Cornwallis Emmanuel Ltd, 1998, 110 pp. How to apply business principles to church leadership. Watts is a member of the International Coalition of Apostles. www.marketsunlocked.com.

Wentroble, Barbara. *You are Anointed: God Has an Extraordinary Plan for Your Life.* Ventura, CA: Renew Books, 2001, 172 pp. Chapter 8 deals specifically with marketplace anointing. Wentroble is a member of the International Coalition of Apostles.

Wolf, Nate. *The Gatekeepers.* Tulsa, OK: Insight Publishing Group, 2002, 121 pp. Good insights on how spiritual gifts operate in the marketplace. Concise, punchy chapters.

Wood, Jan. *Christians at Work: Not Business as Usual.* Scottsdale, PA: Herald Press, 1999, 133 pp. How to invite the Holy Spirit to be with you at work and to show the fruit of the Spirit in your life.

Veith, Gene Edward, Jr. *God at Work: Your Christian Vocation in All of Life.* Wheaton, IL: Crossway Books, 2002, 164 pp. A thoughtful treatment of the Reformation doctrines of Luther relating to our vocation as a divine calling.

Resources by Os Hillman

FREE E-mail Devotional

Start your day by reading an e-mail that encourages you to experience the Lord's presence at work. *TGIF Today God Is First* is a free daily e-mail subscription which has a scripture verse and brief devotional applied to a workplace situation. Subscribe by going to: www.marketplaceleaders.org.

Marketplace Mentor

Twice a month, receive more in-depth Biblical teaching on various topics related to your workplace calling, marketplace tips, proven business principles, and free and discounted resources via this e-mail e-Zine. When you subscribe you'll receive three free e-books by Os Hillman. Only $15 a month or save $30 for an annual $150 subscription.

TGIF Today God Is First

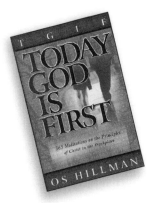

365 Meditations on the Principles of Christ in the Workplace
The daily email devotional in book form! *Today God Is First* provides daily meditations that will help you focus your priority on knowing Jesus more intimately every day. Hardback, 400 pp. B100 $17

TGIF Paperback

180 devotionals presented by topics that range from God's will for your life to adversity. The smaller size and weight allows you to carry it with you wherever you go. Paperback, 286 pp. B101 $14

TGIF Small Group Bible Study

The popular *TGIF Today God Is First* book is now a 12-week, small group Bible study that is ideal for workplace groups. This study includes discussion questions; a workplace application with added scriptures that will allow the leader to extend or reduce the study time.
Booklet, 48 pp. B102 $8

Faith & Work: Do They Mix?

When you have an intimate relationship with Jesus, you will understand that your faith and work are not separate in God's eyes. This book will help you understand why your work IS your ministry.
Paperback, 128 pp. B104 $10

Making Godly Decisions

How can you know if you are making a decision that will be blessed by God? In *Making Godly Decisions*, you will learn the principles for making good decisions that are also godly decisions.
Paperback, 80 pp. B105 $10

The Purposes of Money

Why does God prosper some, while others still live in need? Can we trust God to provide when we don't have enough? In this book you will discover five fallacies of belief that most people live by regarding money. You will also learn the five primary reasons God gave us money.
Paperback, 80 pp. B107 $10

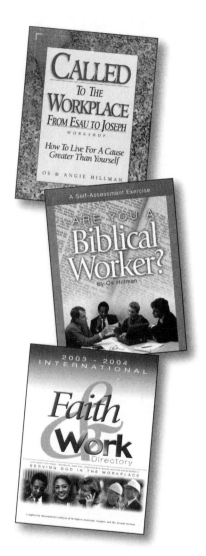

Called to the Workplace: From Esau to Joseph

This is Os and Angie Hillman's complete one-day workshop that helps men and women discover their purpose in work and life. It is loaded with practical application principles to understand God's method of calling, biblical decision-making, and the role adversity plays in every believers life. $49 5 CDs, $15 workbook

Are You a Biblical Worker?

Here's a self-assessment tool to help you discover where you are in your biblical knowledge of applying faith in your workplace. The inventory test features 50 True/False/Sometimes questions and answers. You will be challenged to think through workplace situations that most of us face every day. Biblical texts and case studies support the answers. Great for small group Bible studies. $12.95

2003-2004 International Faith & Work Directory

This alphabetical listing of organizations from around the world that relate to the Christian faith at work movement includes more than 1,200 non-profit ministries, colleges, and churches dedicated to serving God in the workplace. It is compiled as a resource for the faith and work movement and provides a "snapshot" of the movement. $25

MarketplaceLeaders
Helping You Fulfill God's Calling

3520 Habersham Club Drive, Cumming, GA 30041 USA

678-455-6262

Some products are not available in stores.
See our website to order: www.faithandworkresources.com

The International Coalition of Workplace Ministries

(ICWM) is a fellowship of workplace believers who want to ignite leaders for workplace transformation by modeling Jesus Christ. We do this by inspiring, connecting and equipping leaders who want to transform the workplace for Christ. The ICWM website, www.icwm.net, is a clearinghouse for information, resources and organizations in the faith and work movement.

To learn more about our mission and purpose visit our website at www.icwm.net.

Faith and Work Resources.com is your source for the very best in books and audio resources serving the faith and work movement. Visit us at www.faithandworkresources.com

International Coalition of Workplace Ministries
3520 Habersham Club Drive
Cumming, GA 30041 USA
Visit us at: www.icwm.net

227